Instant Pot Pressure Cooker Cookbook

Delicious and Healthy Recipes for Your Electric Pressure Cooker, Eat Real - Lose Weight!

Jennifer West

Table Of contents

- **INTRODUCTION** 9
- **CHAPTER 1: BREAKFAST** 13
  - RECIPE 1: BLUBERRY YOGURT 14
  - RECIPE 2: MUSHROOM OATMEAL 16
  - RECIPE 3: INSTANT POT BARLEY BREAKFAST 18
  - RECIPE 4: JAPANESE-STYLE SWEET POTATOES 20
  - RECIPE 5: GROUND CORN BREAKFAST BOWLS 22
  - RECIPE 6: BREAKFAST BURRITOS 24
  - RECIPE 7: INSTANT POT CHOCOLATE CEREAL 26
  - RECIPE 8: BROWNIE PUDDING 28
  - RECIPE 9: FRENCH TOAST CINNAMON ROLL IN BOWL 30
  - RECIPE 10: POTATO PUFFS BREAKFAST 32
  - RECIPE 11: EGGS IN AVOCADOS 34
  - RECIPE 12: FRUIT BREAKFAST COBBLER 36
  - RECIPE 13: CHOCOLATE MOUSSE 38
- **CHAPTER 2: RICE AND PASTA** 40
  - RECIPE 14: INSTANT POT MAC AND CHEESE 41
  - RECIPE 15: CHICKEN ALFREDO 42
  - RECIPE 16: INSTANT POT SPAGHETTI WITH GROUND BEEF 44
  - RECIPE 17: INSTANT POT ZITI 46
  - RECIPE 18: CASHEW CHICKEN NOODLES 47
  - RECIPE 19: INSTANT POT PRIMAVERA PASTA 48
  - RECIPE 20: COCONUT MANGO RICE 50
  - RECIPE 21: CHICKEN PAELLA 51
  - RECIPE 22: FAJITA PASTA 53
  - RECIPE 23: FAJITA PASTA 55
  - RECIPE 24: INSTANT POT PASTA PIZZA 57
  - RECIPE 25: PESTO PASTA 59
  - RECIPE 26: INSTANT POT TIKKA MASALA PASTA 61
  - RECIPE 27: INSTANT POT LASAGNE 63
  - RECIPE 28: BEEF GOULASH 65
- **CHAPTER 3: VEGETABLES, GRAINS AND BEANS** 67
  - RECIPE 29: INSTANT POT DOUBLE BEANS 68
  - RECIPE 30: INSTANT POT TAGINE 69
  - RECIPE 31: INDIAN-STYLE SAAG 71
  - RECIPE 32: VEGGIE MUSHROOM ROAST 73
  - RECIPE 33: MASHED SWEET POTATOES 75
  - RECIPE 34: STEAMED ARTICHOKES 77
  - RECIPE 35: INSTANT POT GREEN BEANS 79

RECIPE 36: INSTANT POT POLENTA 80
RECIPE 37: INSTANT POT CARROTS WITH ORANGE JUICE 82
RECIPE 38: STEAMED RED CABBAGE WITH APPLE SAUCE 83
RECIPE 39: INSTANT POT RATATOUILLE 85
RECIPE 40: INSTANT POT REFRIED BEANS 87

CHAPTER 4: SOUPS AND STEWS 88

RECIPE 41: BEEF AND BROCCOLI STEW 89
RECIPE 42: FISH STEW 90
RECIPE 43: INDIAN STYLE CAULIFLOWER STEW 92
RECIPE 44: GUINNESS STEW WITH GREEN BEANS 94
RECIPE 45: SPINACH DAL STEW 96
RECIPE 46: GINGER ASPARAGUS STEW 98
RECIPE 47: MUSHROOM AND SAUSAGE STEW 100
RECIPE 48: FENUGREEK STEW 102
RECIPE 49: TUNA STEW 104
RECIPE 50: INSTANT POT TURKEY CHILI STEW 106
RECIPE 51: OKRA STEW 108
RECIPE 52: CHICKEN GARLICKY STEW 110
RECIPE 53: KIMCHI STEW 112

CHAPTER 5: SEAFOOD AND POULTRY 114

RECIPE 54: ROSEMARY TALIPA 115
RECIPE 55: PECAN-CRUSTED SALMON 116
RECIPE 56: SALMON WITH SAUCE MAYONNAISE 118
RECIPE 57: INSTANT POT STEAMED CLAMS 119
RECIPE 58: INSTANT POT OCTOPUS 120
RECIPE 59: INSTANT POT STEAMED SEA BASS 121
RECIPE 60: INSTANT POT CRAB LEGS 123
RECIPE 61: INSTANT POT CHICKEN WITH AVOCADO 124
RECIPE 62: CHICKEN WITH ALMONDS AND MANGO 126
RECIPE 63: BUTTERED CHICKEN 128
RECIPE 64: INSTANT POT SPICY CHICKEN BREAST 130
RECIPE 65: COCONUT CHICKEN WITH LEMONGRASS 132
RECIPE 66: CHICKEN CHILI 134
RECIPE 67: CHICKEN DRUMSTICKS 136
RECIPE 68: CHINESE-STYLE CHICKEN 138
RECIPE 69: CHICKEN MASALA 140
RECIPE 70: CASHEW AND CHICKEN CURRY 142
RECIPE 71: CHICKEN WITH RASPBERRY 144

CHAPTER 6: BEEF, LAMB AND PORK 146

RECIPE 72: PORK WITH CINNAMON AND APPLE 147
RECIPE 73: CRUSTED LAMB WITH DIJON MUSTARD 149
RECIPE 74: INSTANT POT LAMB SHANK 151
RECIPE 75: LAMB KHEEMA 153
RECIPE 76: INSTANT POT LAMB MEATBALLS WITH OLIVE SAUCE 155

RECIPE 77: INSTANT POT CHEDDAR CHEESE SANDWICH ... 157
RECIPE 78: INSTANT POT OXTAILS ... 158
RECIPE 79: BEEF KOFTAS ... 160
RECIPE 80: BEEF VINDALOO ... 161
RECIPE 81: INSTANT POT BHUNA ... 163
RECIPE 82: INSTANT POT LAMB SAUSAGE ... 165
RECIPE 83: SHEPHERD'S PIE ... 166
RECIPE 84: INSTANT POT SWISS STEAK ... 168
RECIPE 85: INSTANT POT LEG OF LAMB WITH VEGETABLES ... 169

CHAPTER 7: TURKEY, GOOSE AND DUCK ... 171

RECIPE 86: INSTANT POT GOOSE ... 172
RECIPE 87: GOOSE BARBACOA ... 174
RECIPE 88: DUCK CONFIT ... 176
RECIPE 89: HONEY GLAZED TURKEY WINGS ... 178
RECIPE 90: INSTANT POT RAGOUT ... 180
RECIPE 91: INSTANT POT DUCK WITH CRANBERRY SAUCE ... 182
RECIPE 92: DUCK TAJINE ... 184
RECIPE 93: INSTANT POT DUCK WITH WALNUTS AND POMEGRANATE ... 186
RECIPE 94: DUCK CHILI ... 188
RECIPE 95: DUCK CURRY ... 190

CHAPTER 8: STOCKS AND SAUCES ... 192

RECIPE 96: MEAT SAUCE ... 193
RECIPE 97: TURKEY STOCK ... 195
RECIPE 98: ONION STOCK ... 197
RECIPE 99: CORN STOCK ... 199
RECIPE 100: SHRIMP STOCK ... 201
RECIPE 101: JAPANESE STOCK ... 202
RECIPE 102: LOBSTER STOCK ... 204
RECIPE 103: DUCK STOCK ... 206
RECIPE 104: FISH STOCK ... 208
RECIPE 105: KOREAN-STYLE STOCK ... 210
RECIPE 106: MUSHROOM BROTH ... 212
RECIPE 107: FENNEL AND CRAB BROTH ... 214
RECIPE 108: SPICY BROTH ... 216
RECIPE 109: DASHI KOMBU ... 217
RECIPE 110: VEGGIE GREEN STOCK ... 219
RECIPE 111: VEGGIE GREEN STOCK ... 221

CHAPTER 9: DESSERTS AND BREAD ... 223

RECIPE 112: BROWNIE PUDDING ... 224
RECIPE 113: CRUMBLED APPLES ... 226
RECIPE 114: INSTANT POT CHOCOLATE COATED PEARS ... 228
RECIPE 115: INDIAN STYLE OBATTU ... 230
RECIPE 116: SWEET HONEY BREAD ... 232
RECIPE 117: WHOLE WHEAT BREAD ... 234

- Recipe 118: Bread with cheese 236
- Recipe 119: Banana Bread 238
- Recipe 120: Pumpkin Bread 240
- Recipe 121: Cranberry Bread 242
- Recipe 123: Cheddar Cheese Bread 244
- Recipe 124: Chocolate Bread 246
- Recipe 125: Apple Bread 248
- Recipe 126: Pumpkin seeds bread 250
- Recipe 127: Cornbread 252

CONCLUSION 254

© Copyright 2020 By Jennifer West All Right Reserved.

In no way it is legal to reproduce, duplicate, or transmit any part of this document by other electronic means or printed format. Any recording of this publication is strictly prohibited, and any storage of this material is not allowed unless with a written permission from the publisher. All rights reserved.

The information provided herein is stated to be truthful and consistent, in that any liability, regarding inattention or otherwise, by any use or abuse of any policies, processes, or directions contained within is the solitary and complete responsibility of the recipient reader. Under no circumstances will any legal liability or blame be held against the publisher for any reparation, damages, or monetary loss due to the information herein, either directly or indirectly.

Legal Notice:

This book is copyright protected. This is only for personal use. You cannot amend, distribute, sell, use, quote or paraphrase any part or the content within this book without the consent of the author or copyright owner. Legal action will be pursued if it is breached

DISCLAIMER NOTICE:

Please only read the information contained within this document is for educational purposes only. Every attempt has been made to provide accurate, up to date, complete and reliable information. No warranties of any kind are expressed or implied. Readers acknowledge that the author is not engaged in the rendering of legal, financial, medical or professional advice.

By reading this document, the reader agrees that under no circumstances are we responsible for any losses, direct or indirect, which are incurred as a result of the use of information contained in this document, including but not limited to errors, omissions, or any inaccuracies

Introduction

What is Instant Pot?

Instant pot means different things to a lot of people. For some people, it is basically a slow cooker. For some other people, it is as the name implies; something that ensures you have your meal instantly. But if you really are focused on getting a direct definition of instant pot, it is safe to say that instant pot is a multi-purpose cooker that allows you to prepare your meals in different ways. Having an instant pot is like having the size of half of your kitchen in just one machine. This is because it has the ability to grill, bake, cook, fry and do so much more at the push of a button.

The popularity of instant pot is so incredible that it is almost hard to believe that they entered the market just a decade ago. 10 years ago you needed to buy different equipment for different purposes in the kitchen. This meant that the idea of having a small but fully functional kitchen was almost next to impossible because you would need the space to put all these equipment. And then this Canadian brand walked in with their invention and it has quickly taken over our kitchen no one is complaining because there are so many advantages to having an instant pot.

But don't think that the invention stopped with the first instant pot (as it is sometimes called) created by the Media group. Actually, there are other brands who have jumped on the wagon and created variations of the original. All of which come with improved benefits. Major culinary brands like Cuisinart and Gourmia have also created products that function the same way as the instant pot. Even the company that came up with the original invention itself has developed newer and better versions of the instant pot. Whether you choose to call it an instant pot, a pressure cooker or a slow cooker, there is one fact you cannot ignore. These kitchen devices are your one-stop spot for all of your cooking needs and you do not need to be a world-class chef to enjoy the meals that can be made in them.

How to Use the Buttons?

For those of us who are not too tech savvy, the idea of utilizing a device that has so many functions and requires the push of a button to activate those functions might seem like a daunting prospect. I mean you are supposed to be able to cook your chicken one minute and then make your cheesecake the other minute. So, how do you switch and ensure that you are able to get the most out of each meal? Well the answer is very simple... you just push a button. However, there are few things you need to take into consideration before you start pushing those buttons.

First of all there are different types of instapots and they all come with different functions. There are those with 7 programmable features and then you have those that go as high as 10. But it doesn't just end there. You also have the plus and minus buttons which help you regulate the pressure and temperature as well as cooking time for the food. The most popular model when it comes to instant pots has to be the Instant Pot Duo 7 in 1 multi-functional electric pressure cooker. There are models that came before and after this one so you may need to refer to the manual of the type that you have if it is different from the one I just mentioned.

Since this one appears to be the preferred choice for most users as well as the most recommended, I'm going to go over the major buttons on this particular model and give you tips on how you can use it. For starters it has seven programmable features which means you can use it to do the following;

Pressure Cooking Button: This button is probably going to be the one that you will use the most as it is very versatile when it comes to meals. You can use it to cook your soup, stew or meat. Use the + and - buttons to regulate the temperature and adjust the time for your cooking. You also want to ensure that you are following the recipe to the letter which means that you need to know whether the food you're preparing has to be made at low pressure or high pressure. Super tip: Add half cup to one cup of liquid to the inner pot in order to pressurize the unit. This is very important.

Sauté Button: This is perfect for those quick and easy meals that you just stir fry in a skillet or a pan. Just press the button, pour in the oil (very little), toss in your stir fry ingredients and you are set to go. This cooking does not require liquid and you can adjust the temperature to suit your needs. Super tip: if you're doing a meal prep, start your stir-fry before you get into the pressure cooking. That way you do not need to clean up the pot before moving to your next meal prep.

Slow Cooker: You use this button for those meals that you want to cook on low heat for a long period of time. Basically it is going to do what your Crock-Pot used to do. This button has a default time of 4 hours but you can adjust it to suit your needs. You can set it in the morning before you leave for the office in such a way that by the time you get back from work, you have a meal ready and waiting for you. Super tip: if you want to shorten the time for a meal that would normally take hours to prepare, use the "less" button.

Steamer: Cooking your vegetables in such a way that they are able to retain the nutrients in them can be very tricky. But not to worry when using the instant pot, that is what this button is for. This feature ensures that your vegetables retain all their essential nutrients while giving you the perfect texture for your meal. Super tip: play System her up inside the pool to prevent your vegetables from getting burnt or stuck to the port

Warmer: Are you done with all of your meal preparation but still want to ensure that your food stays hot until it is ready to be served? I give you the warmer button. It does exactly what it says on the name... it keeps your food warm without compromising flavour or texture. Super tip: This button can also be used as the cancel button when you have initiated a cooking program that you want to stop abruptly.

The other buttons such as rice, multi-grain, porridge, meat, stew, poultry and so on are basically there to prepare meals that fall under that category. You just have to follow the instructions as laid out in the recipe and also pay attention to each meal that you prepare. Experience typically is your best teacher. But most importantly, have fun with process

The Benefits of Instant Pot

There are so many incredible benefits of instant pot and I'm going to list some of them out in a bit. But I want to start out by highlighting what I think is the most amazing benefit that instant pot has to offer... The ability to adapt cooking into your lifestyle. Food is very essential. No matter how busy you are, at some point you will get hungry. The thing is, you may not always have the luxury of eating outside or having someone else prepare a meal for you. Instant pot allows you to enjoy home cooked meals without requiring you to dedicate so much time and knowledge to the process.

That said what is a look at some of the other fantastic benefits;

1. It cuts back your cooking time without compromising the flavour and texture of the food. So, in other words it gives you homemade meals really fast and ensures that it stays fresh.

2. You can cook almost anything in it. The idea that you need to get a particular special equipment for different cooking purposes is fast becoming antiquated. Nobody has that time or wants to spend all that resources when you have a quick and easy all-in-one option.

3. It makes cleaning up after cooking so much easier. When you prepare a full meal, there is a chance that you may have to go through different kitchen appliances in order to get that done. But from defrosting your meal to sauteing, from baking and then slow cooking... everything stays in one unit which leaves you with less washing up to do.

Cleaning Your instant Pot

Since we are on the subject of washing up, let us look at how to keep your instant pot clean and looking brand new. For starters, do not toss the entire thing into a dishwasher right away just because it says it is dishwasher friendly. The inner pot is the one that goes in the dishwasher. The rest will have to be done manually.

So first, unplug your instant pot. Take out the inner pot and wash it manually or put it in the dishwasher like I said earlier. The next step is to use a wet dish cloth to clean the inside and outside of the cooker. After that, you want to use a small sponge or brush or anything that can get into those pesky nooks and crannies of the pot in order to get out dried food residue. This is particularly important if you use this device constantly. And finally, wash the lid of the pot which is the part that gets dirtiest the most with soap and warm water. Don't forget the smaller places where food can get stuck like the quick release handle.

What to Expect From the Rest of This Book

With an instant pot, even the most inept cook can get a decent meal out of it because all you need to do is toss in the ingredients and the pot does the cooking for you. That being said, you still want to be able to enjoy gourmet meals that are delicious and homemade and this book helps you achieve exactly that. You get a variety of instant pot food ideas that only requires you to combine certain ingredients together and enjoy a bust of flavor when it is done.

You may need to put in some work here and there especially when it comes to preparing the ingredients before putting it into the pot. But these are simple ideas and have been created to suit a variety of food preferences. So whether you are vegan or vegetarian or you are craving something a little more exotic, there is something for you in this book.

CHAPTER 1: BREAKFAST RECIPES

Recipe 1: Bluberry Yogurt

TIME TO PREPARE
8 minutes

COOK TIME
10 Minutes

SERVING
3 People

Ingredients

- 2 Cups of blueberries
- ¼ Cup of sugar
- 1 Tbsp of freshly squeezed lime juice
- ½ Teaspoon of balsamic vinegar
- 2 Cups of drained low-fat yogurt
- 1 Tbsp of shelled and finely chopped pistachios

Instructions

1. Combine all together the blueberries, the sugar, the lime juice and the balsamic vinegar.
2. Pour the ingredients into your Instant Pot and press the button boil at high pressure for around 10 minutes.
3. When the timer beeps, quick release the pressure and let it cool for 10 minutes.
4. Spoon ¼ cup of yogurt to the bottom of your yogurt jars.
5. Top the yogurt with 2 Tbsp of blueberry sauce.
6. Make another layer of thick yogurt and top it with blueberry sauce again.
7. Cover the yogurt and let it chill in the fridge before serving.
8. Serve and enjoy your yogurt.

Nutrition Information

Calories: 190, Fat: 1.5g, Carbohydrates: 37g, Dietary Fiber: 0g, Protein: 7g

Recipe 2: Mushroom Oatmeal

TIME TO PREPARE
6 minutes

COOK TIME
25 Minutes

SERVING
4 People

Ingredients

- 2 Tablespoons of butter
- ½ Medium, finely chopped onion
- 2 Garlic cloves
- 1 Cup of steel cut oats
- 1 Can of about 14 ounces can of chicken broth
- ½ Cup of water
- 3 Sprigs of fresh thyme
- ¼ Teaspoon of salt
- 2 Tablespoons of olive oil
- 8 Oz of sliced Crimini mushrooms
- ½ Cup of finely grated smoked gouda
- 1 Pinch of salt and 1 pinch of freshly ground pepper

Instructions

1. Add the butter to your Electric pressure cooker and select the function "Sauté"
2. When the butter is melted; add in the onions and cook while stirring for about 3 minutes
3. Add in the garlic and cook for about 1 additional minute
4. Add the oats and sauté for about 1 minute pot
5. Add the broth, the water, the thyme, and the salt.
6. Lock the lid into place; then select high pressure and set the pressure cooking time to about 10 minute
7. While the oats are cooking, heat a large sauté pan over a medium-high heat until it becomes hot.
8. Add the olive oil and the mushrooms and cook on both sides until it becomes golden
9. When the timer beeps; turn off the pressure cooker and apply the natural pressure release for about 10 minutes; then apply a quick pressure release to relay the remaining pressure if there is any.
10. When the valve drops; carefully remove the lid.

11. Stir in the oats; then stir in the Gouda until it is melted.
12. Stir in the mushrooms; and season with 1 pinch of salt and 1 pinch of ground black pepper
13. Serve and garnish with the thyme leaves.

Nutrition Information

Calories: 135, Fat: 2.7g, Carbohydrates: 23g, Dietary Fiber: 2.5g, Protein: 4.3g

Recipe 3: Instant Pot Barley Breakfast

TIME TO PREPARE
10 minutes

COOK TIME
18 Minutes

SERVING
4-5 People

Ingredients

- 1 Tablespoon of olive oil
- 1 Cup of pearl barley
- ¼ Cup of finely chopped sweet or red or onion
- 4 Cups of liquid, half water and half broth
- ½ Teaspoon of sea salt
- 4 Ounces of turkey ham, finely chopped
- 4 Ounces of baby kale
- 4 Large eggs, cooked

Instructions

1. Start by adding the olive oil to the pressure cooker and set to manual for about 18 minutes.
2. Add in the barley and the onion; then sauté for a couple of minutes
3. Add in the liquid and the salt and lock the lid into its place.
4. While the barley is cooking, chop the ham
5. When the Electric pressure cooker completes its cooking cycle, apply a quick pressure release and if there is so much liquid in the pan; you would want to drain most of it
6. Return your Instant Pot to the function sauté; then add the chopped ham and sauté while stirring from time to time while you are still preparing the eggs
7. When the eggs are perfectly ready, add in the arugula to the Instant pot, and stir very well to combine
8. Scoop the barley into shallow bowls and top with an egg
9. Garnish with Aleppo pepper, ground pepper, fresh

herbs and scallions
10. Serve and enjoy your dish!

Nutrition Information

Calories: 217, Fat: 10g, Carbohydrates: 15g, Dietary Fiber: 3g, Protein: 14g

Recipe 4: Japanese-Style Sweet Potatoes

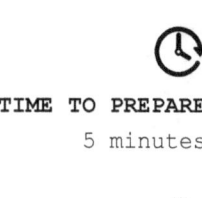

TIME TO PREPARE
5 minutes

COOK TIME
10 Minutes

SERVING
3 People

Ingredients

- 3 roughly-cubed Japanese sweet potatoes
- 1 Lemon with the ends cut off, deseeded and thinly sliced
- 1 Lemon for Zesting
- Chopped fresh herbs, including thyme and oregano
- 2 Tablespoons of Olive or avocado oil
- Sumac
- 1 Pinch of Kosher salt

Instructions

1. Chop the sweet potatoes into small pieces
2. Toss the chopped potato into the steamer basket of your instant pot
3. Poke the potatoes with a knife or a fork
4. Pour in ½ cup of water into the Instant Pot; then seal the lid, and set it for about 10 minutes at a high pressure.
5. While the sweet potatoes are being steaming, thin slice a lemon; then remove the seeds and pick the herbs from the stems
6. When the sweet potatoes are perfectly steamed; carefully release the pressure on your Instant Pot and dump all the water and set it aside
7. Pour enough quantity of oil into your Instant Pot to coat the bottom of the Electric Pressure cooker
8. Select the function sauté and when the oil starts to shimmer; carefully add in the lemon slices and the herbs and stir
9. When the rinds start to become crispy; add in the sweet potatoes while flipping and stirring to your liking
10. Scoop the lemon slices, the potatoes and the herbs

over a plate
11. Sprinkle with salt, additional herbs and sumac
12. Zest over the lemon; then serve and enjoy your breakfast!

Nutrition Information

Calories: 155, Fat: 0.2g, Carbohydrates: 36.7g, Dietary Fiber: 1.9g, Protein: 1.41g

Recipe 5: Ground Corn Breakfast Bowls

TIME TO PREPARE
8 minutes

COOK TIME
25 Minutes

SERVING
4 People

Ingredients

- 1 Cup of stone-ground cornmeal
- 3 and ¾ cups of water
- 1 Cup of 2% reduced-fat milk
- 1 Tablespoon of canola oil
- 1 Chopped garlic clove
- ½ Teaspoon of salt
- ½ Teaspoon of Worcestershire sauce
- 1/8 Teaspoon of ground red pepper
- 4 Ounces of reduced-fat shredded sharp cheddar cheese
- ¼ Cup of chopped scallions

Instructions

1. Combine the cornmeal with about 2 cups of water, the oil, the milk, the garlic in a 4-cup glass measure.
2. Pour the remaining water into an inner pot of your Instant Pot
3. Place a rack the in the bottom of your Electric Pressure cooker
4. Place the 4-cup glass measure over the rack
5. Close the lid of the Instant Pot and lock it in place
6. Turn the steam handle to "sealing" position and press the manual; then select "High pressure" and use the [-] or [+] to choose about 25 minutes
7. When the time is up; turn off the Electric Pressure cooker off
8. Open the Instant Pot using the Pressure Cooker using the Natural Pressure Release method
9. Stir in the salt, the Worcestershire sauce, and the pepper.
10. Gradually add in ¾ cup of the cheese and stir until the cheese melts
11. Spoon the grits into about 4 bowls
12. Garnish with the chopped scallions and the remaining quantity of shredded cheese
13. Serve and enjoy your dish!

Nutrition Information

Calories: 182, Fat: 1 g, Carbohydrates: 38g, Dietary Fiber: 2g, Protein: 4g

Recipe 6: Breakfast Burritos

TIME TO PREPARE
10 minutes

COOK TIME
30 Minutes

SERVING
5 People

Ingredients

For the Egg Base
- 8 Eggs
- ½ Cup of Half and Half
- ½ tsp of Coarse Salt
- ¼ tsp of Pepper
- ½ tsp of Garlic Powder
- 2 Tbsp of chopped Chives
- ¼ Cup of diced Onion
- 1 Cup of chopped cooked Ham
- ¾ Cup of shredded cheese
- ½ Cup of Red Bell Pepper, chopped
- 1 Cup of diced Potato

To Serve

Instructions

1. Pour 1 and ½ cups of water into the inner liner pot of your pressure cooker.
2. Spray a "PIP" pan with cooking spray
3. Add the eggs and the half and half to a large mixing bowl; then whisk all together
4. Add in the remaining ingredients and stir very well them in.
5. Pour the mixture into the PIP pan and cover it tightly with an aluminium foil.
6. Set the pan on the trivet in the bottom of your Instant Pot and lower the pressure cooker.
7. Close the Instant Pot with the lid and close the steam release knob by turning it to the sealing position
8. Press the function button Pressure Cook/Manual button; then use the +/- buttons or dial to select 30 minutes
9. The pot will take just a few minutes to come to pressure.
10. When the cooking time comes to end; apply a

- Flour Tortillas

Quick Release pressure method; by turning the steam release knob to the position Venting

11. Carefully remove the PIP pan from your Instant Pot and carefully remove the aluminium foil
12. Gently stir with a spoon to gently stir and break up the mixture
13. Wrap some of the egg mixture into a flour tortilla to make your breakfast burritos
14. Serve and enjoy your delicious breakfast!

Nutrition Information

Calories: 379.9, Fat: 14 g, Carbohydrates: 41g, Dietary Fiber: 6g, Protein: 21g

Recipe 7: Instant Pot Chocolate Cereal

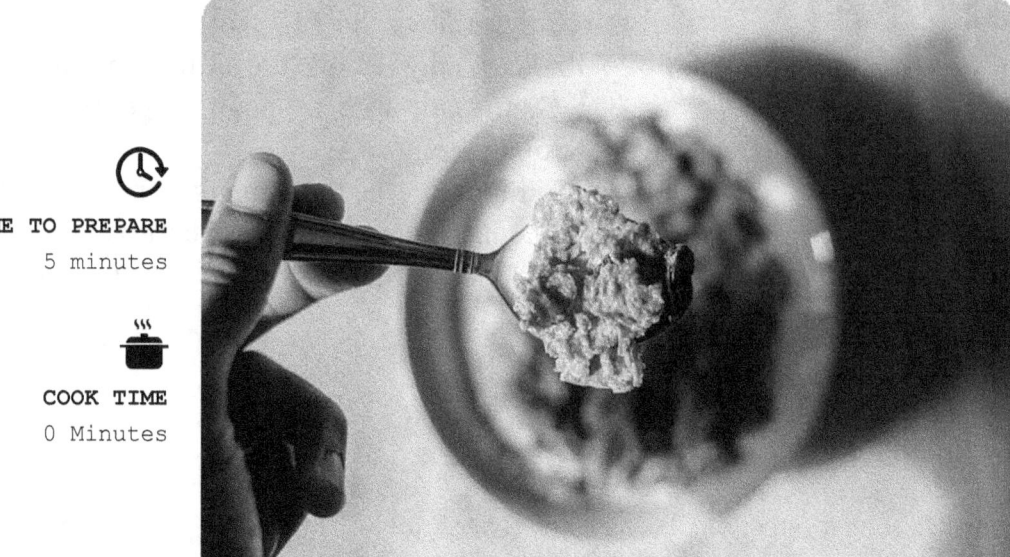

TIME TO PREPARE
5 minutes

COOK TIME
0 Minutes

SERVING
3 People

Ingredients

- 2 cups of full fat coconut milk
- 1 Cup of sugar-free chocolate chips
- 1 Cup of dried unsweetened coconut
- 1 Cup of macadamia nuts
- 1/3 Cup of Swerve confectioner
- ¼ Cup of blanched almond flour
- 2 Tablespoons of unsweetened cocoa powder
- ½ tsp of ground cinnamon
- ½ tsp of kosher salt
- 2 Cups of water

Instructions

1. Set your Instant Pot to the function Sauté; then add in about 2 cups of filtered water
2. Pour in the coconut milk
3. Stir in the chocolate chips, the coconut, the nuts, the Swerve, the flour, the cocoa powder, the cinnamon, and the salt, mix thoroughly.
4. Close the lid of your Instant Pot and set the pressure release to the sealing position
5. Select the manual/pressure cook with high pressure; you should set the timer to 0
6. When the Instant Pot beeps; apply a quick release method by switching the pressure valve to venting position
7. Serve and enjoy your breakfast!

Nutrition Information

Calories: 453, Fat: 44.1 g, Carbohydrates: 19.9g, Dietary Fiber: 8.2g, Protein: 6g

Recipe 8: Brownie Pudding

TIME TO PREPARE
10 minutes

COOK TIME
30 Minutes

SERVING
4 People

Ingredients

- 1 Package of about 18 ounces of dark chocolate brownie mix
- 1 Teaspoon of baking powder
- 2 Large eggs
- 4 Tablespoons of melted butter
- ¼ Cup of milk
- ¼ Cup of brown sugar
- ¼ Cup of cocoa powder
- 8 to 10 store bought caramels
- ¼ Cup of coarsely chopped macadamia nuts, walnuts, or pecans
- ⅓ Cup of boiling water
- Vanilla ice-cream and caramel sauce for

Instructions

1. Spray a cake pan with a non-stick spray
2. In a small mixing bowl, mix altogether the brownie mix with the baking powder
3. In a large mixing bowl; mix the eggs with the butter and the milk until everything is perfectly mixed
4. Add the dry ingredients and mix very well until you get a very well blended batter
5. Scrape your batter into a cake pan
6. In a small mixing bowl, whisk the brown sugar with the cocoa powder; then sprinkle on top of the brownie batter
7. Top with the walnuts and the caramels
8. Pour about ⅓ cup of the boiling water on top of the cocoa powder.
9. Press any dry spots remaining quantity of cocoa powder into the water.
10. Pour about 1 cup of water into your Instant Pot; then place a trivet inside
11. Secure the lid of your Instant Pot and turn the pressure release knob to a sealed position
12. Cook at high pressure for about 30 minutes

serving

13. When the cooking time is complete, use a natural release method and release any remaining pressure
14. Carefully remove the baked cake pan to a wire rack; then let cool for about 5 to 10 minutes
15. Spoon the brownie pudding into bowls and top with vanilla ice cream
16. Drizzle with caramel and 1 pinch of flaky sea salt
17. Serve and enjoy your breakfast!

Nutrition Information

Calories: 172.9, Fat: 2.5 g, Carbohydrates: 43.1g, Dietary Fiber: 3.3g, Protein: 3.4g

Recipe 9: French toast Cinnamon Roll In Bowl

TIME TO PREPARE
15 minutes

COOK TIME
25 Minutes

SERVING
5 People

Ingredients

For the French Toast
- 1 loaf, about 12 slices of sourdough bread, sliced into cubes of about 1 inch each
- 8 Large eggs
- 1 Cup of any type of milk
- 1 teaspoon of vanilla extract
- 2 tablespoons of maple syrup
- ½ Cups of chopped walnuts
- 1 Tablespoon of almond Butter

For the Cinnamon Drizzle:

Instructions

1. Spray a large glass bowl with coconut oil cooking spray.
2. Set the glass bowl aside; and in a small bowl, combine altogether all your ingredients, the almond butter cinnamon drizzle; the consistency of the mixture should be drippy; you can add more coconut oil if needed
3. In a medium bowl, combine the eggs with the milk, the vanilla and the maple syrup
4. Put the bread cubes and half the quantity of the walnuts into the bowl.
5. Drizzle on about half of the quantity of the almond butter cinnamon drizzle over the mixture of the bread
6. Add in the rest of the bread cubes; then sprinkle the rest of the cinnamon and the walnuts on top
7. Pour the egg mixture on top of the mixture

- 2/3 Cup of drippy almond butter
- 2 Tablespoons of maple syrup
- 3 Teaspoons of ground cinnamon
- 1 Tablespoon of melted coconut oil
- Optional Topping
- 4 Tablespoons of chilled butter
- ¼ Cup of brown sugar

and mix the bread cubes with the mixture of the eggs with a spatula
8. Sprinkle over the optional topping
9. Place the metal Instant Pot trivet into the bottom of your Instant Pot and pour in about 1 cup of water.
10. Place the French toast bowl on top of the prepared trivet.
11. Lock the Instant Pot and turn the pressure valve to seal.
12. Press the manual and turn to a high pressure; then cook for about 25 minutes.
13. Apply the quick release method and remove the Instant Pot cover.
14. Let cool; then serve your breakfast with fruit and maple syrup
15. Enjoy!

Nutrition Information

Calories: 368, Fat: 24 g, Carbohydrates: 37g, Dietary Fiber: 3g, Protein: 17g

Recipe 10: Potato Puffs Breakfast

TIME TO PREPARE
12 minutes

COOK TIME
20 Minutes

SERVING
4 People

Ingredients

- 1 Large russet potato
- 1 Medium, finely chopped onion
- 2 Large eggs
- 1 Cup of all purpose or gluten free flour
- 1 Teaspoon of baking powder
- 1 Teaspoon of salt
- ½ Teaspoon of pepper
- 1 Tablespoon of dried parsley, basil or other type of herbs

Instructions

1. Grate or chop a russet potato and chop the onion
2. Add the potato to the bowl of your food processor and blend very well
3. Add the eggs and blend all your ingredients very well
4. Add all your dry ingredients and blend very well until you get a smooth mixture
5. Pour the mixture into egg moulds sprayed with oil
6. Fill each cup to the top and cover with aluminium foil
7. Pour 1 cup of water in the liner of your Electric Pressure Cooker and place the trivet into the bottom
8. Place into the egg mould; then lock the lid on and set the toggle to sealing position
9. Cook on manual/pressure and cook for about 20 minutes. When the cooking process is done; remove and set aside to cool for about 5 minutes
10. In the meantime, place 1 piece of tin foil on cookie sheet and lightly oil it
11. When the puffs are nearly done; turn on an oven to

a broil making sure the rack is close the top of your oven
12. When the puffs have perfectly cooled, run a knife around each of the cups; then invert all the puffs on a cookie sheet and do it carefully
13. Broil for about 10 to 15 minutes
14. Remove the potato puffs to a plate; then put the applesauce into each divot
15. Serve and enjoy your breakfast!

Nutrition Information

Calories: 243, Fat: 11 g, Carbohydrates: 35.5g, Dietary Fiber: 3.2g, Protein: 2.6g

Recipe 11: Eggs in Avocados

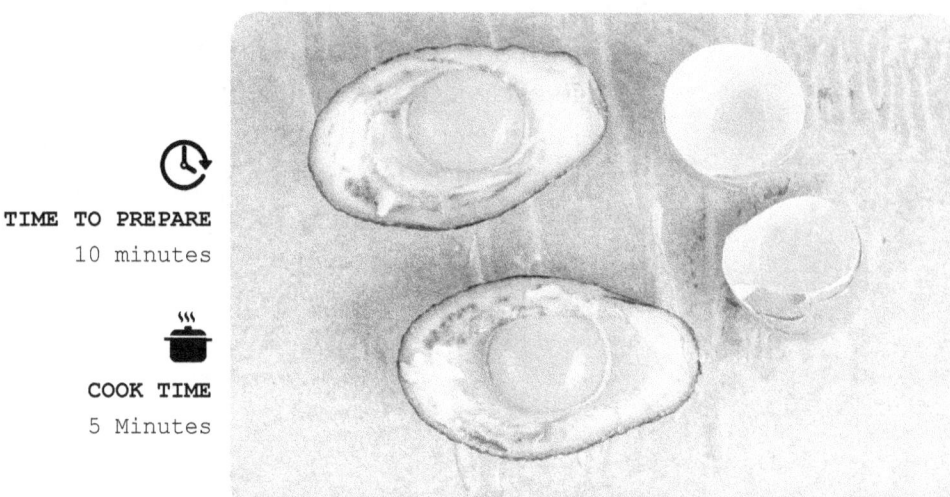

TIME TO PREPARE
10 minutes

COOK TIME
5 Minutes

SERVING
4 People

Ingredients

- 2 Large ripe avocados
- 4 Eggs
- 1 Pinch of sea salt and 1 pinch of black pepper, to taste
- ½ Cup of shredded Cheddar Jack Cheese
- 1/2 Cup of thinly sliced bacon crumbles
- For the optional Garnish:
- Chopped chives or green onions

Instructions

1. Cut the avocados into half lengthwise and remove its pits. With the help of a spoon; carefully remove some of the avocado flesh around its pit so that you create more space for the egg.
2. Reserve the removed flesh for another use or you can smash and season it with 1 pinch of salt and 1 pinch of pepper to taste
3. Top each baked avocado half with a spoonful right before serving
4. Now, place the avocado halves in the steamer basket of your Instant Pot
5. Pour 1 cup of water in your Instant Pot
6. Lower the steaming basket of the Instant Pot with the avocados in the pressure cooker
7. Crack an egg in a measuring cup; then transfer the egg into one of the already prepared avocado halves
8. Repeat the same process with the remaining quantity of the avocado halves and the eggs.
9. Season each avocado half with 1 pinch of salt and 1 pinch of black pepper
10. Top each avocado half with the shredded Cheddar Jack cheese and the crispy bacon pieces.
11. Close the Instant Pot with a lid and lock it into its

place
12. Make sure the vent is sealed and cook on high for about 4 minutes
13. Once perfectly done; apply a quick release pressure method before unlocking the lid
14. Remove the avocados from the Instant Pot and garnish with chopped chives or with green sliced onions
15. Serve and enjoy your breakfast immediately!

Nutrition Information

Calories: 304.3, Fat: 22.5 g, Carbohydrates: 9.6g, Dietary Fiber: 3.0g, Protein: 15.2g

Recipe 12: Fruit Breakfast Cobbler

TIME TO PREPARE
6 minutes

COOK TIME
10 Minutes

SERVING
3 People

Ingredients

- 1 Chopped pear
- 1 Diced apple
- 1 Diced plum
- 2 Tablespoons of local honey
- 3 Tablespoons of coconut oil
- 1/2 tsp of ground cinnamon
- 1/4 cup of unsweetened shredded coconut
- 1/4 cup of pecan pieces
- 2 tbsp of sunflower seeds
- Coconut whipped cream

Instructions

1. Place the cut fruit into the stainless steel bowl of your Electric Pressure Cooker Instant Pot.
2. Add in the honey and the coconut oil; then sprinkle with the cinnamon and secure the lid into its place
3. Make sure the pressure cooker valve is into sealed position
4. Press the Steam button; it displays 10 minutes; then let the fruits cook
5. Quick release the pressure when the pressure cooking cycle is completed
6. Remove the lid and once it is safe to open it; open the lid and transfer the cooked fruit with a spoon to a serving bowl
7. Place the pecans, the coconut and the sunflower seeds into the liquid and press the button "sauté"
8. Press
9. Let the contents cook and shift from time to time so that they won't burn
10. Once the mixture starts browning for about 5 minutes; remove them and top with the cooked fruit
11. Top with the coconut whipped cream

12. Serve and enjoy your breakfast!

Nutrition Information

Calories: 487, Fat: 26.4 g, Carbohydrates: 69.5 g, Dietary Fiber: 21.2g, Protein: 8.6g

Recipe 13: Chocolate Mousse

TIME TO PREPARE
5 minutes

COOK TIME
6 Minutes

SERVING
4 People

Ingredients

- 1 and 1/2 cups of heavy cream
- 1/2 cup of whole milk
- 5 Egg yolks
- 1/4 cup of sugar
- 1 Pinch of salt
- 8 ounces of bittersweet melted chocolate
- 1 Cup of whipped cream
- Grated chocolate for decoration

Instructions

1. Bring the milk and the cream to a boil in a small saucepan
2. In a large mixing bowl, mix altogether the egg yolks with the sugar and the salt
3. Whisk in the chocolate until it is blended; then pour into about 6 custard cups
4. Add about 1 and 1/2 cups of water to your Instant Pot; then place the trivet into the bottom
5. Put 3 cups on top of the trivet and then place another trivet over the cups
6. Stack the remaining cups over the second trivet
7. Lock the lid in its place; then select High Pressure and set the timer for about 6 minutes and when the beep sounds, turn off the pressure cooker and apply a natural pressure release for about 15 minutes
8. Do a quick pressure release method to release any remaining pressure and when the valve drops; carefully open the lid
9. Remove the cups to a wire rack and when cool; wrap with plastic wrap; then refrigerate for about 4

hours
10. Serve and enjoy your breakfast!

Nutrition Information

Calories: 288, Fat: 21.8 g, Carbohydrates: 22.7 g, Dietary Fiber: 2.2g, Protein: 4g

CHAPTER 2: RICE AND PASTA RECIPE

Recipe 14: Instant Pot Mac and Cheese

TIME TO PREPARE
6 minutes

COOK TIME
9 Minutes

SERVING
4 People

Ingredients

- 2 tablespoons of unsalted butter
- 16 ounces of dried pasta shells or elbow macaroni
- 4 Cups of water
- 1/2 teaspoon of kosher salt
- 3 and 1/2 cups of shredded cheddar cheese
- 1/2 cup of half-and-half

Instructions

1. Turn on your Instant Pot to the function sauté; then add in the butter
2. Once the butter is melted; turn your Instant Pot off
3. Add in the pasta, the water and the salt
4. Seal your electric pressure cooker; then use the manual setting to set your Instant Pot for about 6 minutes at a HIGH pressure; then electric pressure cooker will take about 10 minutes to come to pressure
5. When the cook time is done, immediately apply a quick release of pressure.
6. Turn your electric pressure cooker off
7. Open the lid of the pressure cooker; then add in the cheese and the cheese and half-and-half
8. Stir your ingredients until it is very well combined; then cover your pressure cooker and let sit for about 3 minutes
9. Serve and enjoy your dish!

Nutrition Information

Calories: 257| Fat: 7.8g | Carbohydrates: 37.9g | Fiber: 2.3g |Protein: 9g

Recipe 15: Chicken Alfredo

TIME TO PREPARE
8 minutes

COOK TIME
15 Minutes

SERVING
4-5 People

Ingredients

- 2 tablespoons of olive oil
- 2 large boneless and skinless chicken breasts, chopped into pieces of about 1 inch each; about 1 pound
- 4 Minced garlic cloves garlic
- 1/2 Teaspoon of kosher salt
- 2 Cups of water, divided
- 1 Jar of about 15 ounces of Alfredo sauce
- 8 Ounces of dried fettuccine pasta
- 1/2 cup of finely grated Parmesan cheese
- 1/4 Cup of finely chopped fresh flat-leaf

Instructions

1. Turn on your Instant Pot electric pressure cooker to sauté
2. Add in the olive oil and the chicken when the Instant Pot heats up
3. Cook while stirring from time to time until the chicken starts browning for about 2 to 3 minutes
4. Add in the garlic and the salt and cook for about 5 additional minutes
5. Turn off the Instant Pot; then pour in 1/2 cup of water and scrape the bottom of your Instant Pot to loosen any browned bits
6. Add in the Alfredo sauce and stir to combine very well
7. Use both your hands to break the fettuccine into half; then place evenly on top of the Alfredo and chicken mixture; but do not stir starting from this point on
8. Rinse the Alfredo sauce jar with the quantity of water; then pour the water over the pasta; but don't stir
9. Seal your Electric Pressure cooker; then use the manual setting and set the Instant Pot to cook for about 8 minutes under HIGH pressure; it will take

parsley leaves

about 10 to 12 minutes to come up to pressure
10. When the cooking time is done, immediately apply a quick release pressure method; then turn off your electric pressure cooker
11. Open your Instant Pot; then add in the Parmesan and stir to combine
12. Cover your electric pressure cooker again and let sit for about 3 minutes
13. Sprinkle with parsley; then serve and enjoy your dish!

Nutrition Information

Calories: 310| Fat: 17g | Carbohydrates: 23g | Fiber: 2g |Protein: 17g

Recipe 16: Instant Pot Spaghetti with Ground Beef

TIME TO PREPARE
10 minutes

COOK TIME
10 Minutes

SERVING
4 People

Ingredients

- 1 pound of raw ground beef
- 1 Pound of uncooked standard spaghetti noodles uncooked
- 4 1/3 cups of water
- 24 ounces of spaghetti sauce
- 3/4 teaspoon of salt divided
- 1/8 teaspoon of pepper
- 1/4 teaspoon of garlic powder

Instructions

1. Set the Instant Pot to the function sauté, and add the ground beef.
2. Break the beef into chinks with a wooden spoon; then add in 1/2 teaspoon of salt, 1/8 teaspoon of pepper and about 1/4 teaspoon of garlic powder.
3. Cook for about 7 minutes; then remove the inner pot
4. Remove the cooked beef from the Instant Pot; then drain any fat off; you can just use paper towels; but there is no need to rinse the instant pot
5. Once you are sure the outer part of the Instant Pot is clean; place the clean inner pot back into your instant pot
6. Add the water to the Instant pot with the remaining salt; remember to add the ingredients in the same listed order
7. Break the spaghetti noodles into half; then place into the water; do 3 hand fulls; broken into half
8. Use a spoon to make sure the all your ingredients are covered with water
9. Add in the cooked beef back to Instant pot on top of the noodles
10. Pour the pasta sauce over the top and remember not to stir

11. Cover the Instant Pot with the lid: then set to HIGH pressure for about 4 minutes
12. Let the pressure naturally release for about 5 minutes; then release the remaining pressure with the manual release
13. After the indicator of the pressure has lowered, carefully remove the lid
14. Use two tongs to stir very well; then pick apart any stuck pieces
15. Let the spaghetti rest for about 5 minutes; then give a quick stir
16. Serve and enjoy with fresh chopped basil and grated parmesan cheese!

Nutrition Information

Calories: 473| Fat: 25g | Carbohydrates: 26g | Fiber: 6g |Protein: 34g

Recipe 17: Instant Pot Ziti

TIME TO PREPARE
5 minutes

COOK TIME
6 Minutes

SERVING
3 People

Ingredients

- 1 and 1/2 cups of chicken broth
- 1 Cup of heavy cream
- 1 Teaspoon of dried minced garlic
- 1 Pinch of salt and 1 pinch of pepper to taste
- 8 Oz of dry ziti pasta
- 1 Cup of red pasta sauce
- 1 Cup of shredded parmesan cheese
- 1/2 Cup of shredded mozzarella cheese

Instructions

1. Pour the broth, the cream, the garlic, the salt, the pepper and the noodles to your instant pot in this order; make sure not to stir
2. Set your Electric Pressure cooker for about 6 minutes
3. Let the pressure naturally release; then set for about 6 additional quick release method
4. Add the red pasta sauce to your Instant Pot and stir
5. Slowly add in the cheese and stir
6. Serve and enjoy your dish!

Nutrition Information

Calories: 435| Fat: 34g | Carbohydrates: 17g | Fiber: 2g |Protein: 17g

Recipe 18: Cashew Chicken Noodles

TIME TO PREPARE
6 minutes

COOK TIME
6-7 Minutes

SERVING
2-3 People

Ingredients

- 1 cup of chicken broth
- 1/4 cup of brown sugar
- 2 tbsp of soy sauce
- 1/2 tsp of minced dried garlic
- 1/4 tsp of sesame oil
- 1/8 tsp of salt
- 1 Package of Top Ramen
- 1 Cup of cooked, frozen chicken chunks
- 2 Cups of frozen stir fry veggies
- 3/4 cup of cashews

Instructions

1. Pour the chicken broth, the garlic, the cream, the pepper, the salt and the noodles to your Electric Pressure cooker; make sure not to stir
2. Set your Instant Pot Electric Pressure cooker for about 6 to 7 minutes
3. Let the pressure release in a natural way; then set for about 6 quick release additional minutes
4. Add in the red pasta sauce to the Instant Pot and stir
5. Serve and enjoy your dish!

Nutrition Information

Calories: 425| Fat: 21g | Carbohydrates: 52g | Fiber: 0g |Protein: 6g

Recipe 19: Instant Pot Primavera Pasta

TIME TO PREPARE
7 minutes

COOK TIME
13 Minutes

SERVING
3-4 People

Ingredients

- 2 TBSP of olive oil
- 1 cup of roughly chopped Broccolini tops
- 1 cup of thinly sliced and chopped red onion
- 1 Cup of julienned sweet bell pepper
- 1 Cup of roughly chopped asparagus
- 1 Cup of sliced cremini or baby Bella mushrooms
- 1 Cup of sliced cherry tomatoes
- 3 large, finely minced or smashed garlic cloves
- 1 Tablespoon of good Italian seasoning
- 8 oz of penne Rotini or rigatoni
- 4 cups of vegetable broth
- 1/2 cup of freshly shaved pecorino

Instructions

1. Place all of the veggies; starting with the Broccolini to the garlic cloves; then drizzle with 1 tablespoon of olive oil and sprinkle with the Italian seasoning
2. Season with 1 pinch of salt; and make sure all your veggies are evenly coated with seasoning and oil
3. Set the mixture of the ingredients aside
4. Toss the veggies until they are very well coated with oil and seasoning; then set it aside
5. Set your Electric Pressure cooker to the sauté mode; then drizzle in the remaining other 1 tablespoon of olive oil and let it heat up
6. Drizzle in the 1 TBSP of olive oil and let it heat up a little bit
7. Add in the vegetables and let simmer; while stirring for about 5 to 7 minutes and once they become tender, transfer back to a large bowl
8. Cover your ingredients to keep warm, then turn the off the function sauté
9. Pour in the broth and the penne to the Instant Pot: then give a quick stir
10. Lock the lid of the Instant Pot down; then set the valve to a sealing position
11. Cook on a High pressure for about 5 minutes
12. When perfectly done, apply a quick release method
13. Scoop up about 1 cup of the broth: then set it aside
14. Add in the pasta

- Romano or parmesan cheese
- Freshly chopped parsley or basil

15. Drain the rest of the broth; then add the pasta back to the Instant Pot; toss in your vegetables and the reserved broth and give a quick stir
16. Add in the cheese and stir
17. Garnish with freshly chopped parsley or basil
18. Serve and enjoy your dish!

Nutrition Information

Calories: 233.8| Fat: 12.1g | Carbohydrates: 26g | Fiber: 4.4g |Protein: 8.2g

Recipe 20: Coconut Mango Rice

TIME TO PREPARE
4 minutes

COOK TIME
8 Minutes

SERVING
3 People

Ingredients

- 1 Tablespoon of olive oil
- 1 and ½ cups of long-grain white rice
- 1 Can of 14 ounces of unsweetened coconut milk
- 2/3 Cup of water
- 1 Teaspoon of salt
- 1 Large, peeled and diced ripe mango

Instructions

1. Heat your Instant Pot by pressing the button "sauté"; then add in oil and add the rice and coat very well with oil
2. Pour in the coconut milk, the mango, the water and the salt and stir; then close the lid of the Instant Pot and pressure cook for about 7 to 8 minutes at a high pressure
3. When the timer beeps; quick release the pressure; and when it is safe to do, open the lid of the Instant Pot
4. Transfer the rice to a separate dish and fluff it with a fork
5. Serve and enjoy your dish!

Nutrition Information

Calories: 261.2| Fat: 3.9g | Carbohydrates: 54g | Fiber: 1.6g |Protein: 3.7g

Recipe 21: Chicken Paella

TIME TO PREPARE
5 minutes

COOK TIME
13 Minutes

SERVING
3 People

Ingredients

- 1 Tablespoon of olive oil
- 1 Pound of thinly sliced chorizo, chicken sausage
- 1 Heaping cup of white rice
- 1 Teaspoon of saffron
- ¼ Teaspoon of fine sea salt
- 1 Cup of chunky and thick salsa
- 1 Cup of chicken stock
- ½ Cup of chopped roasted red pepper
- 1 Cup of frozen peas
- 1 wedged lemon wedges
  Chopped parsley

Instructions

1. Heat the olive oil in the inner pot or the Instant Pot by pressing the function 'sauté'
2. Add the thinly sliced chicken sausage and cook it for about 5 minutes until the chicken sausages look brown
3. Transfer the chicken sausage to a platter; but do not remove the oil from the Instant Pot
4. Add the white rice, the saffron, the fine sea salt, the thick and the chunky salsa and pour in the chicken stock into the inner pot.
5. Stir your ingredients very well and lock the lid with the vent in sealed position
6. Set the Instant Pot Pressure to "High" and the timer to about 8 minutes
7. When the timer beeps; use the quick release method; then stir in the red pepper, the frozen peas and the chicken sausage; then replace the lid on top and press the button "Keep warm" for about 4 to 5 minutes
8. Stir your ingredients very well
9. Serve and enjoy your chicken paella!

Nutrition Information

Calories: 278.7| Fat: 13.3g | Carbohydrates: 33.2g | Fiber: 4.5g |Protein: 7.6g

Recipe 22: Fajita Pasta

TIME TO PREPARE
4 minutes

COOK TIME
8 Minutes

SERVING
3-4 People

Ingredients

- 1 tbsp of olive oil
- 2 medium-sized chopped chicken breasts
- 1 tbsp of taco seasoning
- 4 Minced garlic cloves
- 1 Finely chopped yellow onion
- 2 Cups of chicken broth
- 2 Cups of fresh salsa
- 1 lb of large pasta shells
- 1 Finely diced red
- 1 Finely chopped yellow pepper
- 1 Finely chopped green pepper

Instructions

1. Add the olive oil, the chicken, the taco seasoning, the garlic, the onion, the chicken broth, the salsa and the shells to your Instant Pot; make sure to leave the shells on top of your ingredients
2. Cook on a high pressure for about 3 minutes; then apply a quick pressure release method
3. Your Instant Pot will take about 10 to 15 minutes to preheat
4. Pressure cook for about 3 minutes
5. Remove the lid of your Instant Pot; then when it is safe to open it, add in the bell peppers; then sour cream and the cheddar cheese and stir very well
6. Replace the lid on top and let sit for about 5 minutes
7. Remove the lid once more and add in the cilantro
8. Top with avocado; then serve the pasta into 6 bowls
9. Serve and enjoy your dish!

- 1 Cup of grated cheddar cheese
- 1/2 cup of sour cream
- 1/3 cup of chopped fresh cilantro
- 1 Diced avocado

Nutrition Information

Calories: 496.1 | Fat: 14.9g | Carbohydrates: 41.5g | Fiber: 5.3g | Protein: 45.6g

Recipe 23: Fajita Pasta

TIME TO PREPARE
4 minutes

COOK TIME
8 Minutes

SERVING
3-4 People

Ingredients

- 1 tbsp of olive oil
- 2 medium-sized chopped chicken breasts
- 1 tbsp of taco seasoning
- 4 Minced garlic cloves
- 1 Finely chopped yellow onion
- 2 Cups of chicken broth
- 2 Cups of fresh salsa
- 1 lb of large pasta shells
- 1 Finely diced red
- 1 Finely chopped yellow pepper
- 1 Finely chopped green pepper

Instructions

10. Add the olive oil, the chicken, the taco seasoning, the garlic, the onion, the chicken broth, the salsa and the shells to your Instant Pot; make sure to leave the shells on top of your ingredients
11. Cook on a high pressure for about 3 minutes; then apply a quick pressure release method
12. Your Instant Pot will take about 10 to 15 minutes to preheat
13. Pressure cook for about 3 minutes
14. Remove the lid of your Instant Pot; then when it is safe to open it, add in the bell peppers; then sour cream and the cheddar cheese and stir very well
15. Replace the lid on top and let sit for about 5 minutes
16. Remove the lid once more and add in the cilantro
17. Top with avocado; then serve the pasta into 6 bowls
18. Serve and enjoy your dish!

- 1 Cup of grated cheddar cheese
- 1/2 cup of sour cream
- 1/3 cup of chopped fresh cilantro
- 1 Diced avocado

Nutrition Information

Calories: 496.1 | Fat: 14.9g | Carbohydrates: 41.5g | Fiber: 5.3g | Protein: 45.6g

Recipe 24: Instant Pot Pasta Pizza

TIME TO PREPARE
10 minutes

COOK TIME
4 Minutes

SERVING
4 People

Ingredients

- 1 lb of Italian Sausage
- 1/2 Chopped Onion
- 1 and 1/2 tsp of Italian Seasoning
- 1/2 tsp of Oregano
- 2 tsp of Garlic Powder or 2 finely minced garlic cloves
- 1/4 - 1/2 tsp of Red Pepper Flakes
- 1/2 tsp of Kosher Salt
- 1/4 tsp of Pepper
- 1 Chopped green or red Bell Pepper
- 6 Oz of sliced mushrooms
- 4 Cups of Low Sodium Chicken Broth
- 16 Oz of Rotini
- 1 Jar of about 24 of Marinara Sauc
- 8 Oz of shredded Mozzarella Cheese

Instructions

1. Turn on your Instant Pot to the setting sauté; then add the onion and the sausage and cook for about 3 minutes
2. Add the Italian seasoning, the oregano, the garlic powder, the red pepper flakes, the salt, the pepper, and the bell pepper
3. Add in the mushrooms and stir.
4. Add in the broth or the water and stir very well; then make sure to scrape the bottom of the pot to deglaze
5. Add in the pasta evenly on top of the mixture; but don't stir
6. Pour the sauce on top of the pasta and cover it very well; but don't stir
7. Cancel the sauté function; then place the lid over the pot and turn the steam release knob to the sealing position
8. Press the pressure cook manual button; then the +/- button or just dial to select 4 minutes for the rotini
9. Cancel the Sauté function and when the cook cycle

- 5 Oz of Pepperoni Slices
- 1/2 Cup of Sliced Black Olives
- 1/2 Cup of Cooked Bacon Pieces
- 1/2 cup of Pineapple Chunks
- Canadian Bacon

is finished, apply a Quick Release of the pressure/steam just by turning the steam release knob to the Venting position.

10. When it is safe to do; open the lid and stir the pasta
11. Add in half of the cheese and about 3/4 of the pepperoni
12. Add in the olives or any other ingredients you like
13. Sprinkle the remaining quantity of cheese on top and arrange the remaining quantity of pepperoni on top
14. Close the lid and let the cheese melt
15. Serve and enjoy your dish!

Nutrition Information

Calories: 287 | Fat: 15.3g | Carbohydrates: 25.7g | Fiber: 4g | Protein: 12.7g

Recipe 25: Pesto Pasta

TIME TO PREPARE
5 minutes

COOK TIME
3 Minutes

SERVING
3 People

Ingredients

- 1 tbsp of olive oil
- 2 medium-sized, chopped chicken breasts
- 3 Minced garlic cloves
- 4 Cups of water
- 1 lb of rotini pasta
- 1/2 tsp of salt
- 1 cup of grated parmesan cheese
- 1 jar of 270mL of store-bought pesto
- 1 chopped red pepper
- 1 Finely chopped small red onion
- 1 Chopped head of broccoli

Instructions

1. Add the olive oil, the chicken, the garlic, the water and the pasta to the Instant Pot in this order and make sure the pasta is submerged below the surface of the water
2. Cook your ingredients on High pressure for about 3 minutes
3. The Instant Pot will take about 15 minutes to preheat; then 3 minutes to pressure cook
4. When the cooking cycle is finished, do a quick release of the pressure; then remove the lid
5. Stir in the salt, the parmesan cheese, the pesto, the red pepper, the red onion and the broccoli and mix very well.
6. Place the lid back; then let sit for about 10 minutes for your veggies to steam
7. Serve and enjoy your dish!

Nutrition Information

Calories: 376 | Fat: 22g | Carbohydrates: 22g | Fiber: 2g | Protein: 21g

Recipe 26: Instant Pot Tikka Masala Pasta

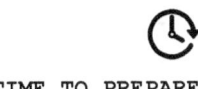

TIME TO PREPARE
5 minutes

COOK TIME
5 Minutes

SERVING
3-4 People

Ingredients

- 1 cup pasta of your choice
- 1 tbsp olive oil
- 1 tsp cumin seeds
- 3 cloves garlic minced
- 1 small onion diced
- 3 small tomatoes chopped
- 1 tsp turmeric powder
- 1 tsp curry powder of choice
- 1 tbsp coriander powder
- red chili powder to taste
- salt to taste
- 1 1/4 cup Water or as needed
- cilantro to garnish

Instructions

1. Put your instant pot on the sauté mode High
2. Add in the oil and let the pressure cooker heat up
3. Add in the cumin seeds and the garlic and sauté both ingredients for a couple of minutes
4. Add the oil and let it get hot.
5. Add cumin seeds and garlic and fry. Add onions and saute well.
6. Add the tomatoes and fry for a few minutes or until the tomatoes become soft
7. Add in all the spice powders together with the salt
8. Fry for about 1 minute or two.
9. Add in the pasta and the water and mix your ingredients
10. Turn off the sauté mode
11. Put your instant pot on the manual mode high for about 5 minutes and keep the vent to sealing position.
12. Apply a quick release or a natural pressure release
13. Garnish with chopped Cilantro
14. Serve and enjoy your delicious dish!

Nutrition Information

Calories: 161 | Fat: 3.9g | Carbohydrates: 26.9g | Fiber: 1.6g | Protein: 33.7g

Recipe 27: Instant Pot Lasagne

TIME TO PREPARE
4 minutes

COOK TIME
9 Minutes

SERVING
4 People

Ingredients

- 1/2 Pound of oven-ready lasagna noodles
- 2 Cups of shredded into large pieces, Mozzarella cheese
- ¼ cup of grated Parmesan cheese
- 2.5 to 3 cups of meat sauce
- 1 Pinch of salt
- 1 Pinch of pepper

For the ricotta Cheese Mixture

- ¾ cup of Ricotta cheese
- 1 teaspoon of Italian seasoning
- 1 large egg
- ⅓ teaspoon of kosher salt

Instructions

1. Start by creating the Ricotta Cheese Mixture
2. In a large mixing bowl, beat one egg; then add in about ¾ cup of Ricotta cheese.
3. Season with 1 tsp of Italian seasoning, the ground black pepper, and about ⅓ tsp of kosher salt.
4. Assemble the Instant Pot Lasagna and to do that Line a 7-inch spring form pan with a parchment paper and break the uncooked lasagna noodles into small pieces
5. Layer the noodles into the bottom of Instant pot in one layer
6. Add the shredded mozzarella cheese on top; then repeat the layering cycle twice
7. Add ¼ cup of the freshly grated Parmesan cheese on the top
8. Wrap the spring form pan with aluminum foil
9. Pour 1 cup of cold water into your Instant Pot
10. Place a trivet into the Instant Pot and create a sling foil within
11. Place the spring form pan over the trivet; ten close the lid of your Instant Pot and pressure cook at a High pressure for about 7 to 9 minutes at a temperature of 425°F
12. For an easier pressure release, use a paring knife to

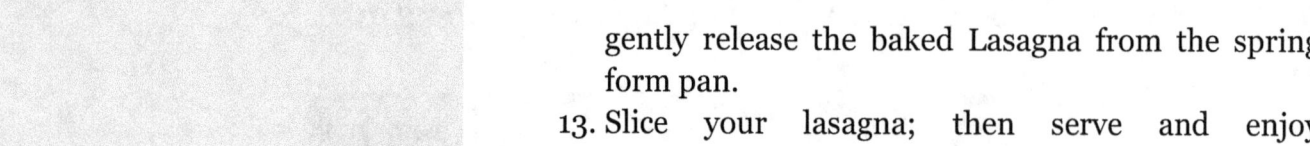

gently release the baked Lasagna from the spring form pan.
13. Slice your lasagna; then serve and enjoy immediately!

Nutrition Information

Calories: 449.2 | Fat: 15.6g | Carbohydrates: 37.3g | Fiber: 3.9g | Protein: 40.2g

Recipe 28: Beef Goulash

TIME TO PREPARE
5 minutes

COOK TIME
4 Minutes

SERVING
5 People

Ingredients

- 1 lb of ground beef
- 1 finely chopped large onion
- 3 garlic cloves
- 2 cans of 15- ounce of tomato sauce
- 2 cans of 15- ounce of chopped tomatoes
- 2 tbsp of Italian seasoning
- 3 tbsp of soy sauce
- 3 cups of elbow noodles
- 2 and 1/2 cups of water
- 2 to 3 bay leaves
- 1 Pinch of salt and 1 pinch of pepper to taste

Instructions

1. Turn your Instant Pot on the function sauté and when hot, add in the ground beef; the garlic, the salt, the pepper, and the onion.
2. Cook until the meat is completely browned.
3. When the meat is browned; drain the fat; then add in the tomato sauce, the diced tomatoes, the Italian seasoning, the soy sauce, the water, the noodles, and the bay leaves.
4. Set your Instant Pot to the manual function button high pressure for about 4 minutes.
5. When the timer is up; do a quick release of pressure.
6. Remove any bay leaves; then stir
7. Top with the Take out bay leaves and give your mixture a good stir.
8. Top with the grated Parmesan Cheese; then serve and enjoy your dish!

Nutrition Information

Calories: 502 | Fat: 16g | Carbohydrates: 63g | Fiber: 5g | Protein: 28g

CHAPTER 3: VEGETABLES, GRAINS AND BEANS RECIPES

Recipe 29: Instant Pot Double Beans

TIME TO PREPARE
6minutes

COOK TIME
20 Minutes

SERVING
3-4 People

Ingredients

- 1 Can of drained garbanzo beans
- 1 Tbsp of lemon juice
- 1Tbsp of olive oil
- 1 Minced garlic clove
- ½ Teaspoon of ground cumin
- ½ Teaspoon of salt
- 2 Drops of sesame oil

Instructions

1. Add your double beans and close the lid of the Instant Pot
2. Set at high pressure for around 17 minutes
3. Once the timer beeps, drain the water and add oil to the Instant Pot
4. Add the asafetida and sauté for 2 minutes
5. Add the curry leaves and the green chilies and sauté for 1 minute on a low heat
6. Add the cooked double beans and the salt and mix the ingredients very well.
7. Remove the beans of the heat and serve it with grated coconut
   Enjoy a tasty and amazing snack

Nutrition Information

Calories: 110.9| Fat: 0.9g | Carbohydrates: 22.2g | Fiber: 9.5g |Protein: 10g

Recipe 30: Instant Pot Tagine

TIME TO PREPARE
5 minutes

COOK TIME
18 Minutes

SERVING
4 People

Ingredients

The spice mixture:
- 1 + 1/2 tbsp ground cumin
- 1 tsp ground cinnamon
- 2 tsp ground turmeric
- 1 tsp ground ginger
- 1/4 tsp ground black pepper
- 1 tsp salt

Mix the spices in a little bowl.

For the marinade

- 1 cup of vegetable stock
- 2 tsp of tamari
- 4 garlic cloves, minced
- 1/4 thumb fresh ginger – see notes
- 16 oz tempeh (2 packs), cubed

Ingredients for the Tagine:

Instructions

1. Add 2 tsp of the spice mix to an instant pot.
2. Add stock, tamari, garlic, and ginger and stir.
3. Add the tempeh and toss to coat. Let marinate for at least 30 minutes.
4. After the marinade, sauté the mixture
5. Add the onion and dry sauté for 5-10 minutes, until a bit translucent. Add the tempeh with the whole marinade and cook for another 3-5 minutes. Add the remaining spice mix and cook for 1 minute more. Add peeled carrots, sweet potato, prunes, apricots, and stock, close the lid and bring to high pressure for 3 minutes.
6. Quick release and let sit for 3 minutes.
7. Remove the lid, stir and add the lemon juice. Transfer to a serving bowl and top with the herbs.
8. Serve and enjoy your tagine!

- 1 large onion; chopped
- 2 big carrots, chopped
- 1 sweet potato, chopped
- 1/2 cup chopped pitted prunes
- 1/2 cup chopped dried apricots
- 2 cups vegetable stock
- 1/2 lemon, juiced
- chopped parsley and/or cilantro

Nutrition Information

Calories: 175.2| Fat: 3.2g | Carbohydrates: 35.1g | Fiber: 8.5g |Protein: 6.8g

Recipe 31: Indian-Style Saag

TIME TO PREPARE
7 minutes

COOK TIME
18Minutes

SERVING
3 People

Ingredients

- 2 tablespoons ghee
- 2 onions, diced
- 4 teaspoons minced garlic
- 2 teaspoons minced ginger
- Spices
- 2 teaspoons salt
- 1 teaspoon coriander
- 1 teaspoon ground cumin
- 1 teaspoon Garam Masala
- ½ teaspoon black pepper
- ½ teaspoon cayenne, adjust to taste
- ½ teaspoon turmeric
- 1 pound spinach, rinsed
- 1 pound mustard leaves, rinsed
- Pinch of Kasoori methi (dried

Instructions

1. Press the "sauté" button on the Instant Pot and add the ghee. Once it melts, add the onion, garlic, ginger and spices to the pot and stir-fry for 2-3 minutes.
2. Add the spinach, stirring until it wilts and there's enough room to add the mustard greens.
3. Secure the lid, close the pressure valve and cook for 15 minutes at high pressure.
4. Naturally release pressure.
5. Remove the lid and use an immersion blender to puree the contents of the pot (or pour the contents into a blender and then add the blended mixture back into the pot).
6. Stir in the dried fenugreek leaves.
7. Serve with ghee!

fenugreek leaves)
- Ghee or butter

Nutrition Information

Calories: 86 | Fat: 7.2g | Carbohydrates: 3.9g | Fiber: 2.9g | Protein: 3.5g

Recipe 32: Veggie Mushroom Roast

TIME TO PREPARE
6 minutes

COOK TIME
20 Minutes

SERVING
4 People

Ingredients

- 1.25 pounds of Yukon gold potatoes, chopped into pieces
- 1 Pound of baby Bella mushrooms
- 2 Large peeled and chopped carrots into pieces
- 2 Cups of frozen pearl onions
- 4 Peeled and minced garlic cloves
- 3 Sprigs of fresh thyme
- 3 Cups of vegetable stock, divided
- 1/2 cup of dry red or white wine
- 3 tablespoons of tomato paste
- 2 tablespoons of vegetarian Worcestershire sauce
- 2 tablespoons of cornstarch
- 1 Pinch of Kosher salt and freshly-cracked

Instructions

1. Add the potatoes, the mushrooms, the carrots, the onions, the garlic, the thyme, about 2.5 cups of vegetable stock, the wine and the Worcestershire together in the bowl of your Instant Pot pressure cooker, and gently toss to combine your ingredients. Close the lid of the Instant Pot and set the vent to "Sealing" position
2. Press the "Manual"; then press the "Pressure" to "High Pressure"
3. Adjust the arrows up/down until the timer reads about 20 minutes
4. Cook; then let the pressure naturally release for about 15 minutes
5. Carefully turn the vent to the button "Venting"; then release any of the extra pressure and remove the lid
6. In a separate bowl, whisk all together the remaining 1/2 cup of vegetable stock and the cornstarch until everything is perfectly combined.
7. Add to the roast mixture, and gently mix to combine very well
8. Cook for about 1 to 3 minutes
9. Garnish with chopped fresh parsley; then serve and enjoy your dish!

- black pepper
- optional garnish ingredients: finely-chopped fresh parsley

Nutrition Information

Calories: 62| Fat: 4.7g | Carbohydrates: 4.3g | Fiber: 1.3g |Protein: 2.1g

Recipe 33: Mashed sweet Potatoes

TIME TO PREPARE
5 minutes

COOK TIME
15 Minutes

SERVING
3 People

Ingredients

- 1 Cup of water
- 1 Pinch of salt
- 3 Pounds of sweet potatoes peeled and chopped into pieces of about 2" x 2"
- 6 Medium garlic cloves
- 1 teaspoon of kosher salt
- 15 turns of freshly ground black pepper
- 3 Tablespoons of vegan butter
- 1 Pinch of ground cinnamon
- 1/4 cup of canned coconut milk
- 1/2 teaspoon of finely chopped fresh rosemary leaves

Instructions

1. Peel the sweet potatoes and cut it into pieces of 2" x 2" pieces.
2. Peel the garlic cloves and finely chop the fresh rosemary leaves.
3. Place the sweet potato pieces into your Instant Pot fitted with a silicone steamer basket insert with water, 1 pinch of salt and with whole garlic cloves.
4. Place the lid on your Instant Pot and set tp "Sealed"
5. Set your Instant Pot to manual normal pressure for about 15 minutes
6. When the pressure cooking process is up; "Quick Release" the pressure by turning the sealed valve
7. Remove the lid and carefully remove the steamed sweet potatoes to a large mixing bowl
8. With the help of a fork or a potato masher, mash the potatoes
9. Add the remaining ingredients, the salt, the ground black pepper, the vegan butter, 1 pinch of cinnamon, the coconut milk and the finely chopped rosemary leaves and keep

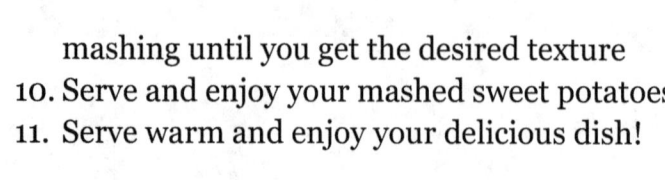

     mashing until you get the desired texture
10. Serve and enjoy your mashed sweet potatoes
11. Serve warm and enjoy your delicious dish!

Nutrition Information

Calories: 204| Fat: 5g | Carbohydrates: 36g | Fiber: 5g |Protein: 3g

Recipe 34: Steamed Artichokes

TIME TO PREPARE
4 minutes

COOK TIME
10 Minutes

SERVING
3-4 People

Ingredients

- 1 cup of water
- 3 garlic cloves
- 1 to 2 bay leaves
- 2 to 4 trimmed fresh large artichokes
- 1 Fresh lemon wedge
- A dipping sauce of your choice

Instructions

1. Pour the water in your Instant Pot; then add the garlic cloves and the bay leaves in your Instant Pot; then place the steamer basket on the bottom of your Instant Pot
2. Rub the lemon wedge on the outside of the trimmed artichokes; then place the artichokes in one layer over the steamer racket in your Instant Pot and toss the lemon wedges in the water below
3. Close the lid of your Instant Pot and set the vent to "sealing" position.
4. Press the "Manual"; then press the "Pressure" until the light on "High Pressure" lights up
5. Adjust the button +/- until the timer read about 10 minutes
6. Use a pair of tongs and remove the artichokes from your Instant Pot; then serve with a dipping sauce of your choice
7. Serve and enjoy!

Nutrition Information

Calories: 64| Fat: 0.4g | Carbohydrates: 13g | Fiber: 7g |Protein: 3.5g

Recipe 35: Instant Pot Green Beans

TIME TO PREPARE
4 minutes

COOK TIME
10 Minutes

SERVING
3 People

Ingredients

- 1 Pound of green beans washed, with the ends trimmed
- Cup of water
- 1 Pinch of desired seasonings

Instructions

1. Pour 1 cup of water into the inner pot of your Electric pressure cooker
2. Place the green beans in the steamer basket of your Electric pressure cooker
3. Set the seal to closed; then set the pressure to High and the manual time to 10 minutes
4. When the pressure cooking time is completed, do a quick release of power
5. Remove the green beans from the Electric pressure cooker
6. Serve and enjoy your green beans!

Nutrition Information

Calories: 35| Fat: 0.4g | Carbohydrates: 7g | Fiber: 3g |Protein: 2g

Recipe 36: Instant Pot Polenta

TIME TO PREPARE
5 minutes

COOK TIME
10 Minutes

SERVING
3 People

Ingredients

- 5 Cups of water
- 1 Cup of polenta/corn grits
- 1 tsp of salt
- 10 ounces of sliced white mushrooms
- 10 Ounces of cherry or of grape tomatoes, halved
- 2 Tbsp of olive oil
- 1 Tbsp of balsamic vinegar
- 1 Tbsp of minced garlic
- 1 Pinch of salt
- 1 Pinch of ground black pepper
- 6 Tbsp of goat cheese

Instructions

1. Add the water, the polenta and the salt to your Instant Pot and whisk.
2. Cover your Instant pot and make sure the valve is in set to sealing position
3. Set the button "Porridge to about 20 minutes on high pressure
4. Turn your oven to a temperature of 400° F and while the polenta is cooking; slice the vegetables; then add the mushrooms, the tomatoes, the oil, the balsamic vinegar and the garlic to a large bowl
5. Toss very well to coat your vegetables ; then add in the mushrooms, the tomatoes, the oil, the balsamic vinegar and the garlic to a large bowl
6. Toss your ingredients very well on a sheet pan
7. Lightly salt and season with 1 pinch of pepper
8. Cook in the oven for about 15 minutes.
9. Once your Instant Pot timer beeps; let the pressure naturally release for about 10 minutes; then move the valve to venting to remove any remaining of pressure
10. Carefully open the lid; then whisk the polenta until it becomes creamy.
11. Scoop the polenta into bowls; then top with

12. Serve and enjoy your delicious meal with 1 tablespoon of goat cheese!

Nutrition Information

Calories: 91| Fat: 0.8g | Carbohydrates: 17.6g | Fiber: 1.4g |Protein: 3.7g

Recipe 37: Instant Pot Carrots with orange Juice

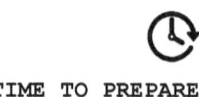

TIME TO PREPARE
5 minutes

COOK TIME
5 Minutes

SERVING
4-5 People

Ingredients

- 2 pounds of medium carrots or baby carrots, chopped into pieces of about 3/4 inches
- 1/2 cup of packed brown sugar
- 1/2 cup of orange juice
- 2 tablespoons of butter
- 3/4 teaspoon of ground cinnamon
- 1/2 teaspoon of salt
- 1/4 teaspoon of ground nutmeg
- 1 tablespoon of cornstarch
- 1/4 cup of cold water

Instructions

1. Combine the carrots with the sugar, the orange juice, the butter, the cinnamon, the salt and the ground pepper in your Instant Pot
2. Lock the lid of your Instant Pot; and make sure the vent is closed
3. Select the manual setting; then adjust the pressure to low and set the time for about 3 minutes and when finished cooking, quick-release the pressure
4. Select the sauté setting and adjust the heat to high
5. Bring your ingredients to a boil; then in a small bowl; mix the cornstarch with the water and gradually stir into the carrot mixture
6. Cook and stir for about 1 to 2 minutes
7. Serve and enjoy your dish!

Nutrition Information

Calories: 187| Fat: 4g | Carbohydrates: 38g | Fiber: 4g |Protein: 2g

Recipe 38: Steamed Red Cabbage with Apple Sauce

TIME TO PREPARE
6 minutes

COOK TIME
3 Minutes

SERVING
3 People

Ingredients

- 1 Medium head of coarsely chopped red cabbage
- 1 Can of about 14 ounces of whole-berry cranberry sauce
- 2 Medium peeled and coarsely chopped
- 1 Medium, chopped onion
- 1/2 Cup of cider vinegar
- 1/4 cup of sweet vermouth, white wine or of unsweetened apple juice
- 1 teaspoon of kosher salt
- 3/4 teaspoon of caraway seeds
- 1/2 teaspoon of coarsely ground

Instructions

1. Combine all your ingredients together; then transfer to your Instant Pot
2. Lock the lid of your Instant Pot and close the pressure cooker release valve
3. Adjust to pressure cook on High for about 3 minutes
4. Let the pressure naturally release for about 5 minutes; then quick release any remaining pressure
5. Serve and enjoy your dish!

pepper

Nutrition Information

Calories: 144| Fat: 0g | Carbohydrates: 34g | Fiber: 4g |Protein: 2g

Recipe 39: Instant Pot Ratatouille

TIME TO PREPARE
7 minutes

COOK TIME
6 Minutes

SERVING
4 People

Ingredients

- 2 medium-size, thinly sliced into rounds heirloom tomatoes
- 2 Thinly sliced into rounds small red onions
- 1 Large zucchini, thinly sliced
- 1 Large, thinly sliced into rounds, squash
- 1 Tablespoon of thyme leaves
- 1 Tablespoon of oregano leaves
- 1 Teaspoon of sea salt
- 1/2 teaspoon of black pepper
- 1/2 cup of marinara sauce, plus more for serving
- 2 large smashed garlic cloves
- 2 tablespoons of olive oil
- 1 Tablespoon of aged balsamic vinegar
- 1 Cup of water

Instructions

1. Sprinkle the vegetable rounds evenly with half the quantity of the thyme, the oregano, the sea salt, and the pepper.
2. Spread the marinara sauce on the bottom of a 6-cup ramekin; then Layer the slices of the tomato, the onion,, the zucchini, the squash and the eggplant
3. Arrange the vegetables in a tight spiral way; start with the outer circle; then add a smaller layer into the idle to fill any of the gaps
4. Once in place, sprinkle the vegetables with the remaining thyme, oregano, the salt, the pepper and the garlic
5. Drizzle with the olive oil and the vinegar
6. Pour the water in the bottom of your Instant Pot; then place a wire trivet in place
7. Place the ramekin on the trivet; and lock the lid; make sure that the steam release handle is set to Sealing
8. Press the manual High pressure and set the timer to about 6 minutes
9. Carefully remove the ramekin; then serve immediately with the marinara
10. Sprinkle with Parmesan and basil; then serve and enjoy your dish!

- Chopped fresh basil
- 1/2 Cup of grated Parmesan, for serving

Nutrition Information

Calories: 104.4| Fat: 5g | Carbohydrates: 15.1g | Fiber: 4.8g |Protein: 2.4g

Recipe 40: Instant Pot Refried Beans

TIME TO PREPARE
5 minutes

COOK TIME
15 Minutes

SERVING
2-3 People

Ingredients

- 1 1/2 cups of dried pinto beans, soaked for an overnight
- 4 oz of pancetta
- 1 tbsp of olive oil
- 3 cups of filtered water
- 1 pinch of salt and 1 pinch of pepper, to taste
- 1/2 tbsp of garlic powder
- 1 tsp of onion powder
- 1 tsp of paprika
- 1/2 tsp of chili powder
- 1/4 tsp of cumin

Instructions

1. Start your Instant pot by pressing the mode sauté; and when hot; add in the oil and the pancetta; then sauté the pancetta for about 5 minutes
2. When the oil heats up; stir very well
3. In the meantime; drain the beans from water and wash thoroughly under water; then add in the beans and the water to the Instant Pot
4. Turn off the sauté function; then close the lid and seal the vent valve.
5. Cook on a high pressure for about 15 minutes and when done, let the pressure naturally release
6. Carefully open your Instant Pot; then season with 1 pinch of salt, the seasoning and the spices
7. Blend the beans with an immersion blender for about 1 to 2 minutes
8. Serve with fresh and chopped cilantro
9. Serve and enjoy your dish!

Nutrition Information

Calories: 237| Fat: 3.2g | Carbohydrates: 39.1g | Fiber: 13.4g |Protein: 13.8g

CHAPTER 4: SOUPS AND STEWS RECIPES

Recipe 41: Beef and Broccoli Stew

TIME TO PREPARE
8 minutes

COOK TIME
45 Minutes

SERVING
4 People

Ingredients

- 1 lb of beef stew meat
- 1 Large quartered onion
- ½ Cup of beef or bone broth
- ¼ Cup of coconut aminos
- 2 Tbsp of fish sauce
- 2 Large minced cloves of garlic
- 1 Teaspoon of ground ginger
- ½ Teaspoon of salt
- 1 Tbsp of Coconuts oil
- ¼ lb of organic broccoli (Frozen)

Instructions

1. In your Instant Pot, place all of your ingredients except for the broccoli.
2. Lock the lid.
3. Now, press the button; Meat/Stew.
4. Let the ingredients get cooked for the preset time of 35 minutes
5. When the timer sets off, press the button off
6. Carefully release the pressure and open the lid
7. Now, add the broccoli to your inner pot
8. This time, place the lid on the instant pot loosely.
9. Let the ingredients simmer for around 15 minutes
10. Serve and enjoy your stew

Nutrition Information

Calories: 206.1| Fat: 10.4g | Carbohydrates: 2.8g | Fiber: 1.5g |Protein: 21g

Recipe 42: Fish Stew

TIME TO PREPARE
5 minutes

COOK TIME
15 Minutes

SERVING
4 People

Ingredients

- 2 to 4 pieces of Study or monkfish (you can also use white fish)
- 1 Medium juiced lime
- 2 tbsp of Coconuts oil
- 1 Large sliced leek
- 1 Seeded and thinly sliced jalapeno
- 3 Minced garlic cloves of garlic
- 2 Cups of halved grape or cherry tomatoes
- 1 Pinch of cayenne
- 1 Teaspoon of chia powder
- 1 Medium can of light coconut milk
- Quinoa and cauliflower for serving
- Micro greens for garnish

Instructions

1. Start by chopping and marinating your fish; then cut it into cubes and set it aside with lime juice in the fridge.
2. In the Instant Pot, press the feature Sauté and sauté your veggies for around 5 minutes
3. Add the coconuts oil and add the jalapeno and the leeks.
4. When the timer sets off; press cancel the sauté button.
5. Add your garlic and the tomatoes; then season with the salt.
6. Add your marinated fish and the lime juice too; then pour the coconut milk, and pour a little bit of water.
7. Stir on a medium heat and add the spices of cayenne with the chia power.
8. Now press the button of Soup/ Stew and taste.
9. Lock the lid and set the timer to 10 minutes.
10. Once the timer goes off, release the steam pressure; then serve your stew with quinoa and enjoy it.

Nutrition Information

Calories: 173.9| Fat: 1.8g | Carbohydrates: 7.2g | Fiber: 1.6g |Protein: 30.6g

Recipe 43: Indian Style Cauliflower Stew

TIME TO PREPARE
7 minutes

COOK TIME
20 Minutes

SERVING
3-4 People

Ingredients

- 2 Tbsp of curry powder
- 1 Teaspoon of Garam Masala
- 1 teaspoon of mustard seeds
- 2 Tbsp of coconut oil
- 1 Large and sliced onion
- 3 Garlic cloves
- 1 Teaspoon of finely grated ginger
- ¾ Teaspoon of fresh ginger
- ¾ Teaspoon of salt
- ½ lb of eggplant
- 4 Cups of cauliflower florets
- 1 Can of diced tomatoes
- ½ Can of rinsed

Instructions

1. Preheat your Instant Pot and pour 1Tbsp of Coconut oil in it.
2. Press the setting feature Sauté and set the timer to 3 minutes.
3. Add the curry powder and the Garam Masala with the mustard seeds and the toast and keep stirring, until you notice the spices start to darken.
4. Cancel the setting Sauté and add the garlic, the ginger and the salt; then add the eggplant, the cauliflowers, the tomatoes, the chickpeas, the water and your reserved spices.
5. Pour in the Coconut milk.
6. Lock the lid of the Instant Pot and let the ingredients simmer.
7. Set your timer to 20 minutes and set the heat to medium.
8. Once the timer goes off; release the pressure and remove the stew from the heat.
9. Serve and enjoy your stew
10. You can top each of the servings with the dollops of yogurt if you want.

- chickpeas
- ½ Cup of water
- ½ Cup coconut milk yogurt
- 1Tbsp of Coconut Oil

Nutrition Information

Calories: 131.4| Fat: 2.7g | Carbohydrates: 21.9g | Fiber: 6.0g |Protein: 5.3g

Recipe 44: Guinness Stew with Green Beans

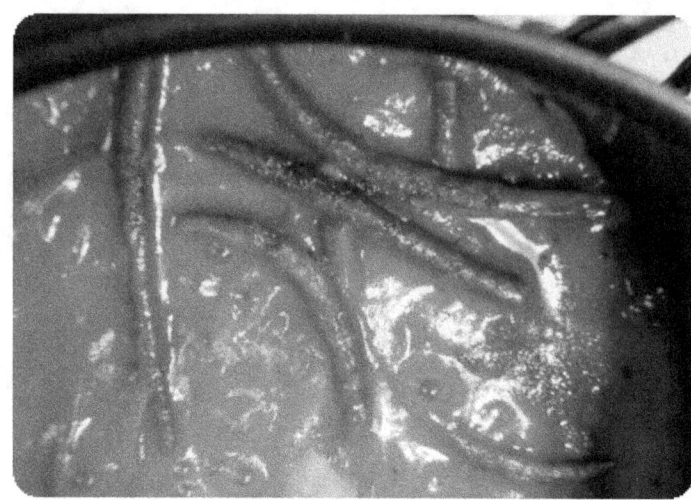

TIME TO PREPARE
6 minutes

COOK TIME
40 Minutes

SERVING
4 -5 People

Ingredients

- 1/3 Cup of Oat flour
- 1 lb of gravy diced beef into small pieces
- ¼ Cup of coconut oil
- 3 Peeled and coarsely cut carrots
- 1 Large halved and coarsely brown onion
- 2 Minced garlic cloves
- 2 Tbsp of tomato paste
- 1 Cup of Guinness beer
- 1 Cup of Campbell's Stock Beef
- 2 Sprigs of fresh thyme
- 2 Bay leaves, dried
- ¼ Cup of coarsely chopped and fresh parsley
- ¼ lb of green beans
- 2 Teaspoons of grated

Instructions

1. Preheat your Instant Pot and pour the coconut oil into it.
2. Meanwhile, put the flour in a large bowl and season it with salt and the pepper; then add the beef to coat it in the mixture.
3. Press the setting feature "Sauté" and set the timer to 5 minutes.
4. Add the beef and cook it for the designated time.
5. After the timer goes off, cancel the Sauté setting and add the carrots, the green beans, the onion and the garlic.
6. After 2 minutes and when you see the ingredients soften, add the paste of the tomato. Pour the Guinness and the stock with the thyme and the bay. Make sure there is enough water.
7. Lock the lid and set the timer to 35 minutes
8. Once the timer goes off, release the pressure and serve it.
9. You can garnish with parsley.

lemon rind

Nutrition Information

Calories: 200.2| Fat: 9.3g | Carbohydrates: 14.4g | Fiber: 3.0g |Protein: 2.6g

Recipe 45: Spinach Dal Stew

TIME TO PREPARE
5 minutes

COOK TIME
15 Minutes

SERVING
4 People

Ingredients

- 2 Tbsp of coconut oil
- 2 medium red or yellow chopped onions
- 3 Minced garlic cloves
- 1 Teaspoon of ground cumin
- 1 Teaspoon of ground coriander
- 1 Teaspoon of ground turmeric
- ¼ Teaspoon of dried cayenne pepper
- ¼ Teaspoon of Flax seeds
- 1 Cup of red lentils
- ½ Cup of yellow peas
- 3 Cups of warm water
- ½ Teaspoon of salt
- 2 Diced medium

Instructions

1. Pour the coconut oil into the Instant Pot and to cook at a medium heat and press the button setting Sauté.
2. When the oil becomes hot, place the cut onions and keep cooking it until it softens.
3. Add the garlic and cook for around 3 minutes.
4. Turn off the medium heat and press the button "Cancel" To cancel the use of the sauté mode.
5. Add the flax seeds, the coriander, the turmeric and the cayenne; then mix it very well to combine it.
6. Add the quantity of lentils, the water, the salt and the tomato wedges; then stir it into the mixture of the onion.
7. Now, cover your Instant Pot with its lid, and make sure the valve is placed into a sealed position.
8. Press the button "Manual" and set the cooking time you need for around 10 minutes.
9. After that program is complete; then press the button 'Cancel' to shift to the warming mode; then wait for 10 minutes before releasing the pressure
10. Add spinach with the cilantro and serve it with

- tomatoes
- 4 cups of spinach
- ¼ Cup of chopped fresh cilantro
- 2 Teaspoons of butter
- Yogurt and fresh cilantro for garnish

brown rice.

Nutrition Information

Calories: 210| Fat: 15g | Carbohydrates: 14 g | Fiber: 3.0g |Protein: 8g

Recipe 46: Ginger Asparagus Stew

TIME TO PREPARE
6 minutes

COOK TIME
35 Minutes

SERVING
3-4 People

Ingredients

- 8 oz of diagonally sliced thin asparagus
- 2 Tbsp of hoisin sauce
- 1 and ½ teaspoons of rice wine
- 1 teaspoon of sesame oil
- 1 Tbsp of coconut oil
- 1 teaspoon of sesame seeds
- 1 teaspoon of chia powder
- 2 teaspoons of minced and fresh peeled ginger
- 2 minced garlic cloves
- 3 medium coarsely cut carrots
- 1/2 teaspoon of coarse salt
- ½ Cup of coconut milk.

Instructions

1. In your Instant Pot, pour the coconut oil with ½ cup of water and add the asparagus.
2. Press the button Sauté in the setting and set the timer to 5 minutes
3. When the timer sets off, cancel the button Sauté and add the rest of the ingredients.
4. Lock the lid of the Instant Pot and set the timer to 35 minutes.
5. Let the ingredients boil and when the timer goes off; release the pressure
6. Serve and enjoy your stew!

Nutrition Information

Calories: 123.3| Fat: 4.4g | Carbohydrates: 16.3 g | Fiber: 4.1g |Protein: 4.7g

Recipe 47: Mushroom and sausage stew

TIME TO PREPARE
10 minutes

COOK TIME
20 Minutes

SERVING
4-5 People

Ingredients

- 2 Tbsp of coconuts oil
- 1 lb of ground turkey or you can use pork sausage
- 1 large chopped white onion
- 3 Minced garlic cloves
- 3 medium sweet, skinned and chopped potatoes
- 10 oz of sliced mushrooms
- 5 Cups of chicken broth
- 1 Cup of dry white wine
- 2 Tbsp of apple cider vinegar
- 1 Tbsp of dried basil
- 1 teaspoon of sea salt
- ½ teaspoon of fresh ground pepper

Instructions

1. In your Instant Pot, select the function Sauté and heat it for 1 minute
2. Pour in the coconuts oil; then add the ground sausage.
3. Sauté the sausage for around 5 minutes
4. Add in the onions and cook for 2 more minutes
5. Add into the Instant Pot the sweet potatoes, the mushrooms, the chicken broth, the wine, the vinegar, the dried basil, the salt, and the pepper, the ginger and the flax seeds.
6. Lock the lid and select the manual to cook for high pressure for around 9 minutes.
7. When the timer goes off; select the button cancel and apply a quick pressure release.
8. Finally, open the lid and add the kale.
9. Let the stew cook with the lid kept open for 3 more minutes or until you see the kale is finally softened but do not let it wilt
10. Serve your stew and garnish with the thyme.

- 3 Cups of roughly chopped kale
- 2 Tbsp of freshly chopped thyme
- 1 Teaspoon of ground ginger
- 1 Teaspoon of flax seeds

Nutrition Information

Calories: 205| Fat: 8g | Carbohydrates: 16.3 g | Fiber: 2.2g |Protein: 12g

Recipe 48: Fenugreek Stew

TIME TO PREPARE
5minutes

COOK TIME
15 Minutes

SERVING
4 People

Ingredients

- 4 Cups of chicken broth
- 1 Cup of coconut milk
- 4 Cups of uncooked egg noodles
- 4 Cups of frozen broccoli florets
- 1/2 Cup of shredded Asiago cheese
- 2 diced carrots
- ¼ Teaspoon of salt
- ¼ Teaspoon of garlic powder
- ½ Cup of cubed butter
- 1 Tbsp of canola oil
- 1Tbsp of Coconut oil
- 1 Teaspoon of Fenugreek
- ½ Cup of chick peas

Instructions

1. In your Instant Pot, pour the coconut oil, add the broth, the fenugreek, the chickpeas, and the noodles.
2. Add the broccoli and the coconut milk; then press the Manual Stew/ Soup
3. Add the rest of the ingredients
4. Lock the lid and set the timer to 15 minutes
5. Once the timer sets off; release the pressure and add ¼ cup of cheese with the garlic power and let the broth boil for 5 minutes
6. Serve and enjoy your stew!

Nutrition Information

Calories: 218.2 | Fat: 4.1g | Carbohydrates: 34.9 g | Fiber: 14.8g | Protein: 12.8g

Recipe 49: Tuna Stew

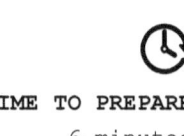

TIME TO PREPARE
6 minutes

COOK TIME
20 Minutes

SERVING
4-5 People

Ingredients

- 1 and ½ lb of fresh tuna steak diced into cubes of 1 inch each.
- 2 diced avocados
- 1/3 Cup of red diced onion
- 1/3 Cup of thinly sliced scallions
- 1 diced large potato
- 2 cut carrots
- 4 Tbsp of Coconut oil
- 1 Tbsp of sesame oil
- 2 Zested and juiced limes
- 1 Teaspoon of sriracha
- 2 Teaspoons of soy sauce
- 1 pinch of sea salt
- 1 pinch of freshly ground pepper
- 1and ½ cups of

Instructions

1. Start by preparing the quinoa and set it aside.
2. Heat the Instant Pot on a medium heat.
3. Pour 1 tbsp of coconut oil and place it into the Instant Pot and press the sauté setting feature.
4. After 2 minutes, press the cancel button and sprinkle the ingredients with the use of sea salt and the ground pepper.
5. Add the onions and the slices of the scallions, the potatoes and the carrots with 2 cups of coconut milk.
6. Lock the lid of the Instant Pot and set the timer to 20 minutes high pressure.
7. Meanwhile, cut your avocados, and combine it with 2 tbsp of coconut oil; 1 tbsp of olive oil and sesame oil with the lime zest; the soy sauce and the sriracha.
8. Once the timer sets off, release the pressure and add the avocado with the red onions and pour the stew on your cooked quinoa.
9. Serve and enjoy your stew!

cooked quinoa

Nutrition Information

Calories: 156| Fat: 5g | Carbohydrates: 15 g | Fiber: 6g |Protein: 14g

Recipe 50: Instant Pot Turkey Chili Stew

TIME TO PREPARE
5 minutes

COOK TIME
15 Minutes

SERVING
4 People

Ingredients

- 1 pound of ground turkey or ground beef
- 1 Chopped onion
- 2 Minced garlic cloves
- 2 Cups of chicken broth
- 1 medium chopped green pepper
- 1 Can of 14 oz of crushed tomatoes
- 1 can of 14.5 oz of fire roasted salsa style chopped tomatoes
- 1 can of 16 oz of rinsed and drained kidney beans
- 1 Can of 15 oz of rinsed and drained black beans
- 1/4 cup of uncooked

Instructions

1. Turn on your instant pot by pressing the setting sauté
2. Add in the ground turkey; then break it up with the help of a wooden spoon.
3. Brown the turkey meat for about 2 minutes; then add in the onions and the garlic and sauté for about 5 minutes
4. Pour in the broth, the green pepper, the crushed tomatoes, the fire roasted tomatoes, the kidney beans, the black beans, the quinoa, the corn, the tomato paste, the chili powder, the cumin, the salt, the pepper and the garlic powder.
5. Cover the Instant Pot and lock the lid; then make sure the valve is set to the "sealing" position and set the manual pressure cook button to about 5 minutes on a High Pressure
6. When the timer beeps; let the pressure naturally release for about 10 minutes
7. Move the valve to the venting position and when you can; open the Instant Pot
8. Stir your chili and season with 1 pinch of salt and

- rinsed quinoa
- 1 can of 16 oz of drained corn
- 1 can of 6 oz of tomato paste
- 1 and 1/2 tsp of chili powder
- 1 1/2 tsp of cumin
- 1 tsp of salt
- 1/2 tsp of pepper
- 1/4 tsp of garlic powder

For the toppings: chopped green onions, grated cheddar, corn chips and sour cream

ground pepper
9. Add in more chili powder
10. Add in the cumin, the salt and the pepper.
11. Ladle into bowls; then serve topped with the desired toppings.
12. Serve and enjoy your chili stew!

Nutrition Information

Calories: 210| Fat: 4.8g | Carbohydrates: 28 g | Fiber: 7.4g |Protein: 16.9g

Recipe 51: Okra Stew

TIME TO PREPARE
6 minutes

COOK TIME
15 Minutes

SERVING
4 People

Ingredients

- 1/4 cup of Water
- 2 tablespoons of Apple Cider Vinegar
- 1 cup of chopped onions
- 1 tablespoon of Minced Garlic
- 14.5 ounces of Canned Tomatoes
- 1 tablespoon of vegetable, chicken, or beef bouillon
- 1 teaspoon of Smoked Paprika
- 1/4 to 1/2 teaspoon of Ground Allspice
- 1 teaspoon of salt
- 1 1/2 pounds of okra fresh or frozen
- 1 tablespoon of lemon

Instructions

1. Place all of your ingredients following the same provided order except for the tomato paste and the lemon juice in the inner liner of your Instant Pot
2. Start with the liquid; the onions and the spices at the bottom of your Instant Pot; then add in the spices at the bottom of your Instant Pot
3. Place the okras on top and cook on High pressure for about 2 minutes
4. Release the remaining pressure; then open the lid; add in the tomato paste and the water; as well as the lemon juice
5. Stir very well serve and enjoy your dish!

juice
2 tablespoons of Tomato Paste

Nutrition Information

Calories: 85| Fat: 8g | Carbohydrates: 19 g | Fiber: 6g |Protein: 4g

Recipe 52: Chicken Garlicky Stew

TIME TO PREPARE
6 minutes

COOK TIME
15 Minutes

SERVING
4 People

Ingredients

- 6 pieces of chicken
- 2 Medium potatoes
- 1/2 an onion
- A quarter of red pepper
- 1 Pinch of salt
- 1 pinch of pepper
- 1 level tsp of turmeric
- 1 level tsp of smoked paprika
- 1 Quarter tsp of garlic and of herb grind
- 1 Teaspoon of chicken spice Robertson
- 1 tbsp of olive oil
- 1 Tablespoon of tomato
  2 tbsp of thick vegetable soup

Instructions

1. Start your Instant, by pressing the setting "sauté"; then add in the chicken to brown it; then add in the paprika and the turmeric on the side facing up
2. Turn the chicken; then add in the garlic, the herbs and the spices
3. Close the lid of the Instant Pot and set the temperature to high for about 5 minutes
4. Add in the onion and the red pepper to let brown
5. Stir very well; then add in the potatoes and close the lid of your Instant Pot; set the timer to 10 minutes and the temperature to High.
6. When the timer beeps, quick release the pressure; then when it is safe to do it, open the lid of your Instant Pot and add a little bit of sugar
7. Add the soup, the salt and the pepper and stir very well
8. You can add a little quantity of pepper; then stir very well
9. Serve and enjoy your dish!

Nutrition Information

Calories: 171.2| Fat: 2.7g | Carbohydrates: 4.2 g | Fiber: 1.2g |Protein: 21.8g

Recipe 53: Kimchi Stew

TIME TO PREPARE
7 minutes

COOK TIME
20 Minutes

SERVING
4-5 People

Ingredients

- 1 tbsp of sesame oil
- 4 Oz of sirloin pork; (thinly sliced)
- 1 Thinly sliced small onion
- 3 Minced garlic cloves
- 1 Teaspoon of Gochujang; Korean chili paste
- 1 Cup of roughly chopped Napa cabbage
- ½ Cup of Kimchi juice
- 1½ cups of water
- 6 Oz of firm tofu, chopped
- 3 Diagonally sliced green onions

Instructions

1. Heat the sesame oil in your Instant Pot, by pressing the setting "sauté"
2. When the oil heats up; add in the pork and fry for about 2 to 3 minutes
3. Add in the onion and sauté for about 2 to 3 minutes Add in the garlic, the gochuhang and the napa cabbage Kimchi and heat for about 3 minutes
4. Pour in the kimchi juice and about 1½ cups of water.
5. Close the lid of your Instant Pot and set the timer for about 15 minutes
6. When the pressure cooking time is up; add in the sliced tofu and cook for about 5 additional minutes by pressing the setting sauté
7. Add the sliced tofu and cook for about 5 additional minutes
8. Add the sliced green onions; then serve immediately with the steamed rice.
9. Serve and enjoy your Kimchi stew!

Nutrition Information

Calories: 186| Fat: 9g | Carbohydrates: 10 g | Fiber: 2g |Protein: 16g

CHAPTER 5: SEAFOOD AND POULTRY RECIPES

Recipe 54: Rosemary Talipa

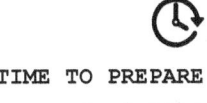

TIME TO PREPARE
4 minutes

COOK TIME
10 Minutes

SERVING
3 People

Ingredients

- 3 Talipa fillets
- 1 tablespoon olive oil
- 2 tablespoons fresh rosemary chopped
- 2 cloves garlic minced
- 1 Pinch salt and freshly ground black pepper

Instructions

1. Put 1 tablespoon of rosemary in the bottom of a bowl.
2. Arrange the cod fillets in one layer.
3. Season with garlic, salt and black pepper and pour the olive oil.
4. Arrange the bowl in the Instant Pot and lock the lid.
5. Set the Instant Pot to "Manual" mode for 5 minutes at high pressure
6. When the pressure cooking cycle ends up; quickly release the pressure
7. When it is safe to do, open the lid of the Instant Pot
8. Serve and enjoy your dish!

Nutrition Information

Calories: 124| Fat: 0g | Carbohydrates: 1g | Fiber: 0g |Protein: 25g

Recipe 55: Pecan-crusted Salmon

TIME TO PREPARE
5 minutes

COOK TIME
10 Minutes

SERVING
4 People

Ingredients

- 3 Tbsp of Dijon mustard
- 3 Tbsp of melted butter
- 5 teaspoons of honey
- ½ Cup of fresh bread crumbs
- ½ Cup of finely chopped pecans
- 3 Teaspoons of chopped fresh parsley
- 6 Fillets of salmon
- 1 Pinch of salt
- 1 Pinch of pepper
- 6 lemon wedges

Instructions

1. Start by heating your Instant Pot over a medium heat.
2. Pour 2 tbsp of vegetable oil in the Instant Pot.
3. In a deep bowl, mix all together the bread crumbs, the pecan and the parsley.
4. Season the salmon very well with the salt and the pepper.
5. Brush the salmon with honey and mustard; then add the pecan on top
6. Cover the salmon with the mixture of the bread crumbs and tightly seal the aluminum foil from all its sides.
7. Place the salmon in the Instant Pot and close the lid.
8. Set at high pressure for 10 minutes.
9. Once the timer beeps, quick release the pressure
10. Serve with lime wedges and enjoy a delicious dish

Nutrition Information

Calories: 353.2| Fat: 24.8g | Carbohydrates: 1.7g | Fiber: 1.1g |Protein: 25g

Recipe 56: Salmon With sauce mayonnaise

TIME TO PREPARE
5 minutes

COOK TIME
10 Minutes

SERVING
3 People

Ingredients

- 3 lbs of salmon fillets
- 1 Cup of mayonnaise
- 1 Tbsp of fresh dill
- 1 Tbsp of lemon juice
- 1 Pinch of salt
- 1 Pinch of ground black pepper

Instructions

1. Combine all of your ingredients together except for the salmon and stir very well.
2. Add a little bit of salt with a pinch of pepper.
3. Place your Instant Pot over a medium heat and pour 2tbsp of vegetable oil.
4. Add the salmon to the Instant Pot and season it generously with pepper and salt.
5. Press sauté and cook the salmon for around 10 minutes; make sure to flip from time to time.
6. Pour the mayonnaise over the salmon and sauté for 5 more minutes.
7. Serve and enjoy your salmon with salad and lime wedges!

Nutrition Information

Calories: 518| Fat: 29g | Carbohydrates: 14g | Fiber: 0g |Protein: 47g

Recipe 57: Instant Pot Steamed Clams

TIME TO PREPARE
5 minutes

COOK TIME
4 Minutes

SERVING
3 People

Ingredients

- 3 lb of clams
- 1 cup of white wine melted
- ½ cup of lemon juice
- ½ cup of melted butter
- 3 Garlic cloves
- 1 Pinch of salt and 1 pinch of pepper

Instructions

1. Carefully clean the clams.
2. Pour the melted butter in your Instant Pot, then add in the garlic cloves and press the setting "Sauté".
3. Cook for about 1 minute until the garlic starts to brown; then remove it from the Instant Pot.
4. Add the white wine and cook for about 2 additional minutes.
5. Add the clams, the lemon juice and 1 pinch of salt.
6. Cook at a high pressure for about 2 minutes.
7. Naturally release the pressure; then release naturally; then remove the lid
8. Serve and enjoy the clams topped with the sauce.

Nutrition Information

Calories: 130| Fat: 2g | Carbohydrates: 4g | Fiber: 0g |Protein: 22g

Recipe 58: Instant Pot Octopus

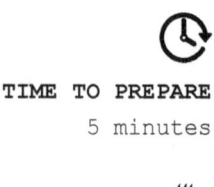

TIME TO PREPARE
5 minutes

COOK TIME
20 Minutes

SERVING
4 People

Ingredients

- 1 Whole rinsed octopus
- 1 Medium, chopped, peeled and halved onion
- 3 Finely minced garlic cloves
- 1 Pinch of kosher salt to taste
- 1 Dash of Spanish paprika to taste
- Extra virgin olive oil for drizzling

Instructions

1. Add the octopus to the instant pot.
2. Add enough quantity of water to cover the octopus.
3. Add onion, the garlic and the salt.
4. Close the lid of your instant pot.
5. Set your instant pot to "Manual" at a high pressure for about 15 minutes; then naturally release the pressure naturally through the steam vent.
6. If the octopus becomes tender; take it out of the Instant Pot; otherwise; you can set the Instant Pot for an additional 5 minutes; then naturally release the pressure through the steam vent
7. Serve and enjoy your dish!

Nutrition Information

Calories: 185| Fat: 2.4g | Carbohydrates: 5g | Fiber: 0g |Protein: 33.7g

Recipe 59: Instant Pot steamed Sea bass

TIME TO PREPARE
5 minutes

COOK TIME
6 Minutes

SERVING
3-4 People

Ingredients

- 1 tsp of minced garlic
- 1 tsp of fresh minced ginger
- 2 tbsp of rice wine
- 1 tbsp of soy sauce
- 1 tbsp of fish sauce
- 1 Pinch of freshly ground black pepper
- 1 lb of whole sea bass
- 2 cups of water
- 1 tsp of fresh ginger, finely julienned
- 1/4 Cup of light soy sauce
- 1 tbsp of water
- 1 Julienned scallion
- 1/4 cup of canola oil

Instructions

1. Start by preparing the marinade and to do that, add all your ingredients, except for the fish and the water in a dish and mix very well
2. Add the fish and mix very well; then set aside for about 20 to 30 minutes
3. In the bottom of your Instant Pot, place a steamer basket in; then pour in the water
4. Put the fish in the steamer basket and secure the lid; then turn to "Seal" position
5. Cook on "Manual" after setting the pressure to Low for about 2 minutes
6. Secure the lid of your Instant Pot and turn to the "Seal" position.
7. Cook on the "Manual" with "Low Pressure" for around 2 minutes.
8. Press the button "Cancel" and apply a quick release.
9. In the meantime; add the ginger, the soy sauce; the wine and 1 tablespoon of water; then mix very well
10. Carefully remove the lid of your Instant Pot and transfer the cooked fish to a serving platter
11. Put the ginger over the fish; then arrange the scallion on top of the fish
12. In a frying pan, add the oil over a medium high heat and cook for a couple of minutes
13. Pour the oil over the fish; then serve and enjoy your

 dish!

Nutrition Information

Calories: 125| Fat: 2.6g | Carbohydrates: 0g | Fiber: 0g |Protein: 23.9g

Recipe 60: Instant Pot Crab Legs

TIME TO PREPARE
5 minutes

COOK TIME
6 Minutes

SERVING
3-$ People

Ingredients

- 2 lb of frozen crab legs
- 3/4 cup of water
- 4 tbsp of melted butter
- lemon juice to taste

Instructions

1. Pace the trivet in your instant pot.
2. Place the crab legs over the trivet.
3. Add the water into your Instant Pot and close the lid
4. Set your Instant Pot to the button "Manual" at a High pressure for about 2 minutes; then release the pressure quickly through the steam vent
5. Open the lid of your Instant Pot; then place the crab legs over serving plates
6. Mix the lemon juice and the butter
7. Drizzle the lemon juice and the butter over the crab legs; then serve and enjoy your dish!

Nutrition Information

Calories: 300| Fat: 4g | Carbohydrates: 1g | Fiber: 0g |Protein: 61g

Recipe 61: Instant Pot Chicken with Avocado

TIME TO PREPARE
8 minutes

COOK TIME
36 Minutes

SERVING
5-6 People

Ingredients

- 4lb of organic chicken
- 1 Tbsp of Coconut Oil
- 1 Teaspoon of paprika
- 1 and ½ cups of Pacific Chicken Bone Broth
- 1 Teaspoon of dried thyme
- ¼ teaspoon of freshly ground black pepper
- 1 teaspoon of ginger
- 2 Tbsp of lemon juice
- ½ Teaspoon of sea salt
- 6 cloves of peeled garlic
- 1 Avocado

Instructions

1. In a medium bowl, combine the paprika, the thyme, the salt, the dried ginger and the pepper. Ten rub the seasoning over the outside of your chicken.
2. Heat the oil in your Instant Pot to simmering
3. Add the chicken breast with its side down and cook it for 6 minutes.
4. Now, flip your chicken and then add the broth, the lemon juice and the garlic cloves.
5. Lock the lid of your Instant pot and set the timer to 30 minutes at high pressure.
6. Meanwhile prepare the avocado cream by whisking the content of the avocado with 2 tbsp of coconut oil and ½ teaspoon of salt and salt.
7. Once the timer beeps, naturally release the pressure.
8. Remove your chicken from the Instant Pot and set it aside for around 5 minutes before serving it.
9. Serve and enjoy your Chicken dish!

Nutrition Information

Calories: 373.6| Fat: 19.8g | Carbohydrates: 8.8g | Fiber: 6.5g |Protein: 40.8g

Recipe 62: Chicken with almonds and mango

TIME TO PREPARE
6 minutes

COOK TIME
10 Minutes

SERVING
3-4 People

Ingredients

- 3 to 4 boneless and skinless chicken breasts
- 2 Tbsp of chicken seasoning
- 1tbsp of fresh ginger
- ¼ Cup of coconut oil
- 3 Tbsp of lime juice
- For the Salsa of the Mango Pepper: 2 cups of diced fresh mangos + 1 cup of diced red bell pepper + 3 tbsp of minced red onion + 1 tbsp of lime juice + 2 Tbsp of minced fresh cilantro +1 pinch of salt + 1 pinch of pepper to taste

Instructions

1. Place your Instant Pot on a medium high heat and pour 2 cups of water into it
2. Place the trivet or the steaming basket in the Instant Pot
3. Trim the excess quantity of fat from your chicken, rinse it and pat dry it; if you need to. Cut the chicken into cubes
4. Place your chicken into a plastic bag and add the seasoning to it; the oil and the lemon juice. Then seal the bag.
5. Once you placed the chicken in the steaming basket, close the lid and press the steam feature on a high pressure for 10 minutes.
6. Meanwhile, combine the ingredients of the mango salsa and season it with oil, salt and pepper.
7. Once the timer beeps, make a quick release of pressure and serve your chicken with mango salsa, sprinkle almond halves; enjoy!

Nutrition Information

Calories: 431| Fat: 13g | Carbohydrates: 49g | Fiber: 4.9g |Protein: 32g

Recipe 63: Buttered Chicken

TIME TO PREPARE
5 minutes

COOK TIME
8 Minutes

SERVING
5 People

Ingredients

- 9 boneless and skinless chicken thighs
- 2 cups of diced tomatoes with its juice
- 3 Seeded and chopped jalapeno peppers
- 2 Tbsp of peeled and chopped fresh ginger root
- ½ Cup of unsalted butter
- 2 Teaspoons of ground cumin
- 1 Tbsp of paprika
- 2 Teaspoons of kosher salt
- ¾ Cup of heavy cream
- ¾ Cup of Greek yogurt
- 2 Teaspoons of Garam Masala
- 2 Teaspoons of ground roasted cumin seeds

Instructions

1. Cut the chicken into cubes or quarters. Put the tomatoes, the jalapeno and the ginger into a food processor and blend all of the ingredients.
2. Add a little bit of butter to the Instant Pot, select the sauté function.
3. When the butter is completely melted, add the chicken and cook for 3 minutes.
4. Remove the chicken into a bow and set it aside.
5. Add the ground cumin and the paprika to the butter into your Instant Pot and cook all together for 1 minute.
6. Add the tomatoes, the salt, the cream, the yogurt and the chicken.
7. Stir and cover the lid of the Instant Pot; then set high pressure for around 5 minutes.
8. When the timer beeps, naturally release the pressure for around 10 minutes.
9. Add the Garam Masala and the roasted cumin and combine the ingredients together; then press sauté to boil for 3 minutes.
10. Serve and enjoy with rice and garnish with cilantro.

- 2 Tbsp of cornstarch
- 2 Tbsp of water
- ¼ Cup of minced cilantro

Nutrition Information

Calories: 355| Fat: 23g | Carbohydrates: 14g | Fiber: 2g |Protein: 23g

Recipe 64: Instant Pot Spicy Chicken Breast

TIME TO PREPARE
6 minutes

COOK TIME
10 Minutes

SERVING
3-4 People

Ingredients

- 1-2 pounds chicken breasts or thighs
- 1 teaspoon sea salt
- 1 onion, diced
- 1 tablespoon avocado oil, lard, or ghee
- 5 garlic cloves, minced
- 1/2 cup organic chicken broth or homemade
- 1 teaspoon dried parsley
- 1/4 teaspoon paprika
- 1 large lemon juiced
- 3-4 teaspoons (or more) arrowroot flour

Instructions

1. Turn your Instant Pot onto the sauté feature and place in the diced onion and cooking fat
2. Cook the onions for 5-10 minutes or until softened. You can also choose to cook until they start to brown
3. Add in the remaining ingredients except for the arrowroot flour and secure the lid on your Instant Pot
4. Select the "Poultry" setting and make sure your steam valve is closed
5. Allow the cooking time to complete, release steam valve to vent and then carefully remove lid
6. At this point you may thicken your sauce by making slurry
7. To do this remove about 1/4 cup sauce from the pot, add in the arrowroot flour, and then reintroduce the slurry into the remaining liquid
8. Stir and serve right away. This also reheats well as leftovers

Nutrition Information

Calories: 170| Fat: 6g | Carbohydrates: 1g | Fiber: 1.9g |Protein: 25g

Recipe 65: Coconut Chicken with Lemongrass

TIME TO PREPARE
6 minutes

COOK TIME
10 Minutes

SERVING
3-4 People

Ingredients

- 1 thick stalk fresh lemongrass, papery outer skins and rough bottom removed, trimmed to the bottom 5 inches
- 4 cloves garlic, peeled and crushed
- 1 thumb-size piece of ginger, peeled and roughly chopped
- 3 tablespoons coconut aminos
- 1 teaspoon five spice powder
- 1 cup full-fat coconut milk (+¼ cup optional)
- 10 drumsticks, skin removed (or 2 pounds

Instructions

1. Peel, trim, and smash the piece of lemongrass. (If you need to read up on cooking with lemongrass, check out this tutorial.)
2. Combine the lemongrass, garlic, ginger, fish sauce, coconut aminos, and five-spice powder into a blender or food processor. Pour in the coconut milk and blitz until a smooth sauce forms.
3. Put the chicken drumsticks into a large bowl and season with salt and pepper. Toss the chicken parts with the salt and pepper.
4. Plug in your Instant Pot and press the "Sauté" button to heat up the insert.
5. Drop in a teaspoon of ghee or coconut oil. When it melts, add the sliced onions. Stir-fry the onions until they're translucent (3-5 minutes).
6. Add the drumsticks to the pot and pour the marinade on top.
7. Press the "Cancel/Warm" button on the Instant Pot and lock the lid with the top dial pointed towards

- boneless, skinless chicken thighs)
- 1 teaspoon Diamond Crystal kosher salt
- ½ teaspoon freshly ground black pepper
- 1 teaspoon ghee or coconut oil
- 1 large onion, peeled and thinly sliced
- ¼ cup fresh cilantro, chopped
- Juice from 1 lime (optional)

8. Press the "Manual" or "Pressure Cook" button and set it to cook for 15 minutes under high pressure. Decrease the cooking time to 10 minutes if you're using boneless, skinless thighs. (If you're using a stovetop pressure cooker, lock the lid and increase the heat to high to bring the contents to high pressure. Once high pressure is reached, decrease the heat to low or enough to maintain high pressure. Set a timer for 15 minutes as your chicken cooks under high pressure.)
9. When the stew finishes cooking, turn off the pressure heater and release the pressure valve. Once the pressure drops, unlock the lid and taste for seasoning.
10. If needed, add a few splashes of fish sauce, a dash of salt, or a grind or two of black pepper. Plate and serve!

Nutrition Information

Calories: 375| Fat: 13g | Carbohydrates: 17g | Fiber: 1g |Protein: 47g

Recipe 66: Chicken Chili

TIME TO PREPARE
6 minutes

COOK TIME
10 Minutes

SERVING
3-4 People

Ingredients

- 2 bone-in Chicken Breasts
- 2 tablespoons Organic Grass-Fed Butter ghee or coconut oil
- 1 teaspoon chili powder
- 2 teaspoons cumin
- 1 pinch Crushed Red Pepper Flakes
- 1 1/2 teaspoons Sea Salt
- 1/2 teaspoon Organic White Pepper
- 1 teaspoon Organic Garlic Powder
- 1 teaspoon Organic Onion Powder
- 1/2 large Organic Yellow Onion chopped
- 2 ribs celery chopped
- 1/2 green pepper chopped

Instructions

1. Liberally season chicken breasts with seasoning.
2. In a large Dutch oven or heavy bottomed pot, heat butter over medium heat. Place chicken breasts, skin side down in pot and lightly brown (2-3 minutes)
3. Turn chicken breasts over (bone side down); add onions, celery and peppers.
4. Sauté until soft, 2-3 minutes.
5. Add water bring to a simmer. Cover and turn heat to low and cook for 1 hour.
6. Remove chicken breasts from liquid, allow to cool
7. Remove skin and bones (discard or freeze use in bone broth next time you make it) roughly chop or shred chicken meat and add back into soup.
8. In a small bowl or cup, whisk together potato starch and about 1/4 cup of the liquid from the soup until smooth. Add into the soup and stir well to combine.
9. Allow thickener to cook in for 2-3 minutes then turn off heat and stir in coconut milk.
10. Serve in bowls topped with chunks of avocado. It is also delicious served overtop of rice

- 1/2 red pepper chopped
- 4 cups Water, filtered
- 2 tablespoon potato starch
- 1 cup organic coconut milk

Nutrition Information

Calories: 226| Fat: 8g | Carbohydrates: 19.6g | Fiber: 6.1g |Protein: 19.72g

Recipe 67: Chicken Drumsticks

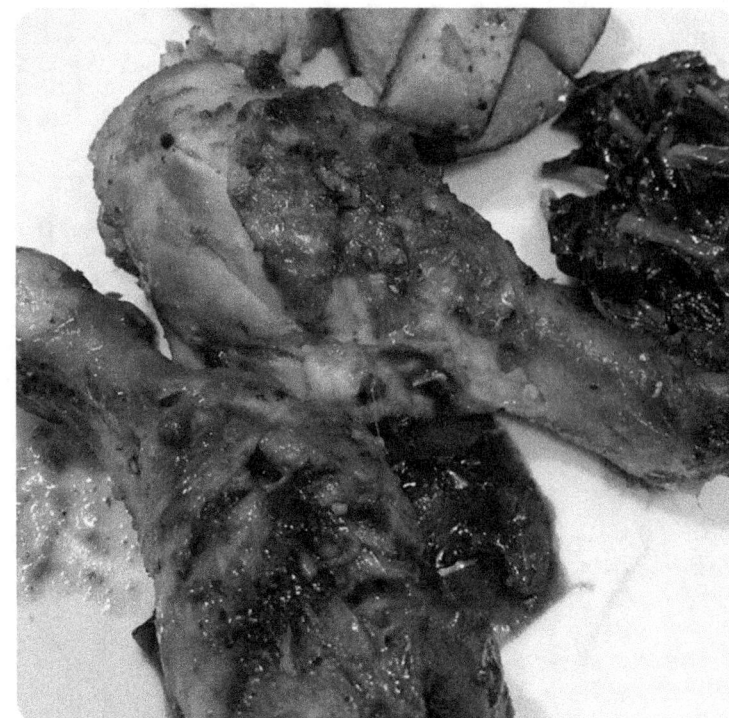

TIME TO PREPARE
7 minutes

COOK TIME
30 Minutes

SERVING
4 People

Ingredients

- 2 lbs chicken leg quarters or drumsticks
- 1 tablespoon of olive oil
- 1 medium onion, thinly sliced
- 3 cloves garlic, minced
- 1 red bell pepper, thinly sliced
- 3 tbsp paprika
- 1/2 cup chicken stock
- 1 tbsp arrowroot
- 1 tbsp fresh lemon juice
- 1/2 cup sour cream
- 1 tbsp parsley, chopped

Instructions

1. Turn Instant Pot to sauté and while Instant Pot is heating, take chicken and trim skin and fat.
2. Season chicken liberally with salt and pepper on both sides and set aside.
3. Drizzle in about a tablespoon of olive oil.
4. Place chicken in Instant Pot and brown, about 3 minutes per side. Remove chicken and place on a plate.
5. Add the onions and garlic and sauté for 2 minutes. Then add in the sliced red bell pepper and continue to cook, another 2 minutes.
6. Add in 3 tablespoons of paprika and stir well to coat.
7. Stir in 1/2 tsp salt; then pour in the chicken broth and scrape up any browned bits with a wooden spoon.
8. Place chicken in the Instant Pot and nestle down

- salt and pepper, to taste

into the liquid; then turn sauté feature off and pressure cook on high pressure for 20 minutes
9. Let pressure naturally release for 10 minutes, and then turn the valve to release the rest of the pressure.
10. Remove about a 1/4 cup of the liquid and mix in the arrowroot (or cornstarch) and pour back into the pot. Turn on sauté and stir slowly until the liquid thicken.
11. Add in the lemon juice. Turn off sauté; then slowly mix in the sour cream.
12. Stir in half the parsley; adjust the salt and pepper
13. Serve over hot egg noodles, rice, or mashed potato and enjoy!

Nutrition Information

Calories: 264| Fat: 15.3g | Carbohydrates: 0g | Fiber: 0g |Protein: 29.6g

Recipe 68: Chinese-Style Chicken

TIME TO PREPARE
5 minutes

COOK TIME
15 Minutes

SERVING
3 People

Ingredients

- 1 pound boneless skinless chicken breasts, sliced into strips
- 1/2 cup chicken broth
- 1/4 cup coconut aminos
- 2 tablespoons sesame oil
- 1 teaspoon fish sauce
- 1 1-inch knob ginger, crushed
- 2 cloves garlic, minced
- 1/4 teaspoon fine sea salt
- 1/4 teaspoon black pepper
- Optional: red pepper flakes, as desired
- 1/4 teaspoon apple cider vinegar
- 10-12 ounces of broccoli florets, about 5-6 cups
- Sesame seeds, for garnish
- Slurry:

Instructions

1. Place chicken in the insert of your Pressure Cooker/Instant Pot.
2. Add in broth, coconut aminos, sesame oil, fish sauce, ginger, garlic, salt and pepper.
3. Cook on manual, high pressure for 8 minutes.
4. Turn the knob to quick release.
5. Add in the slurry and mix to combine.
6. Press off, and then turn on the sauté function. Add in the broccoli on sauté for about 5 minutes, stirring often, or until broccoli has softened and sauce has reduced slightly and thickened. Add apple cider vinegar and mix (this won't add any vinegar taste, just brings out the flavor in the sauce).
7. Garnish and enjoy.
8. Serve with cauliflower rice or white rice!

- 2 tablespoons arrowroot or tapioca flour
- 2 tablespoons water

Nutrition Information

Calories: 190| Fat: 4g | Carbohydrates: 6g | Fiber: 2g |Protein: 36g

Recipe 69: Chicken Masala

TIME TO PREPARE
5 minutes

COOK TIME
15 Minutes

SERVING
3 People

Ingredients

- 1 1/2 tablespoons olive oil
- 1 small onion, finely diced
- 3 cloves garlic, minced
- 1 (2-inch) piece fresh ginger, peeled and grated
- 1/2 cup chicken broth, divided
- 1 1/2 tablespoons Garam Masala
- 1 teaspoon smoked paprika
- 1/2 teaspoon ground turmeric
- 1/2 teaspoon kosher salt
- 1/4 teaspoon cayenne pepper (optional)
- 1 1/2 pounds boneless, skinless chicken thighs, cut into 1 1/2-

Instructions

1. Sauté the aromatics; then set an electric pressure cooker to the sauté feature.
2. Add in the oil and heat until shimmering but not smoking.
3. Add the onion and sauté until softened, about 3 minutes. Add the garlic and ginger and cook until soft and fragrant. The mixture might stick a little to the bottom of the pot; this is normal.
4. Deglaze and add spices: Add 1/4 cup of the chicken broth. Cook, gently scraping the bottom of the pot with a wooden spoon to loosen any stuck-on bits, until the chicken broth reduces by half. Add the Garam Masala, paprika, turmeric, salt, and cayenne pepper, and stir to combine.
5. Add the chicken, broth
6. Add the chicken and stir to combine. Add the remaining 1/4 cup of chicken broth
7. Pressure-cook: Close and lock lid. Pressure-cook for 10 minutes at HIGH pressure. When cooking time is complete, do a quick release of the pressure.

inch pieces
- 1/2 cup coconut milk
- Fresh cilantro, chopped

Add the creamy element
8. Stir the coconut milk into the sauce.
9. Top with chopped cilantro.

Nutrition Information

Calories: 358| Fat: 14.8g | Carbohydrates: 32.5g | Fiber: 9.3g |Protein: 18.8g

Recipe 70: Cashew and Chicken Curry

TIME TO PREPARE
5 minutes

COOK TIME
15 Minutes

SERVING
3 People

Ingredients

For marinating
- 6-7 boneless skinless chicken thighs
- 2 tbsp curry paste
- 3 tbsp coconut milk

For the curry
- 1 tbsp olive oil
- 1 large onion finely sliced into half moons
- 1 bay leaf
- 2 whole black cardamoms
- 1 tsp Garam Masala
- 4 tbsp whole rounded, blanched cashews
- 250 ml unsweetened almond milk
- 2 tbsp cashew butter optional
- To finish
- 2-4 tbsp fresh

Instructions

1. Mix the curry paste and coconut milk together well then rub into the chicken. Refrigerate for at least an hour but most often, I leave them in the fridge overnight.
2. Place the Instant Pot into sauté mode and add the oil. Fry the onions until they soften and start to color then add in the bay leaf and black cardamoms
3. Sprinkle over the Garam Masala then add the chicken thighs and all their marinade. Cook for a couple of minutes for the first side then flip over, add the whole cashews and almond milk.
4. Place the lid on; ensure the nozzle is set to "sealing" and using manual mode, set 10 minutes.
5. Do a quick release when finished cooking, take the lid off and place the IP into sauté once again.
6. Break the chicken thighs up with a large slotted spoon then remove from the pot leaving the watery sauce behind. Stir frequently and reduce to your desired texture - at this point you can stir in the optional cashew butter and beat it well to help thicken the sauce.
7. When reduced add the chicken back in and sprinkle

coriander chopped
- Salt to taste

with coriander before serving

Nutrition Information

Calories: 257| Fat: 13g | Carbohydrates: 14g | Fiber: 3g |Protein: 23g

Recipe 71: Chicken with Raspberry

TIME TO PREPARE
6 minutes

COOK TIME
9 Minutes

SERVING
2-3 People

Ingredients

- 2 Boneless and cubed chicken breasts
- ¼ Teaspoon of salt
- ¼ Teaspoon of pepper
- ½ Teaspoon of ginger
- 2 Tbsp of Coconut oil
- 1 Large and sliced onion
- 1 Cup of chicken broth
- 3 Tbsp of raspberry vinegar
- ¾ Cup of quick cooking rice
- ½ Cup of fresh raspberries

Instructions

1. Sprinkle the chicken with the salt, the ginger and the pepper.
2. Heat the oil in the Instant pot and brown your chicken cubes by pressing the Sauté featuring function.
3. Add the onions, the chicken and the vinegar.
4. Pour ¼ cup of water or you can use coconut milk instead
5. Close the lid of the Instant Pot. Set the feature to high pressure and the heat to low.
6. Cook the chicken for 5 minutes; and once the timer beeps, release the pressure, the chicken and press keep warm.
7. Now, bring the liquid to boil setting function and add the rice.
8. Remove the Instant pot from the heat and set it aside for 4 minutes.
9. Add your cooked chicken and the raspberries.
10. Serve and enjoy your chicken!

Nutrition Information

Calories: 178.9| Fat: 1.4g | Carbohydrates: 13.7g | Fiber: 0.4g |Protein: 26.4g

CHAPTER 6: BEEF, LAMB AND PORK RECIPES

Recipe 72: Pork with Cinnamon and Apple

TIME TO PREPARE
5 minutes

COOK TIME
20Minutes

SERVING
4 People

Ingredients

- 2 lb of boneless pork loin roast;
- 3 medium apples, peeled and sliced;
- ¼ cup of honey
- 1 red onion, halved and sliced;
- 1 tbsp of ground cinnamon;
- 1 cup chicken stock;
- Cooking fat;
- Sea salt and freshly ground black pepper

Instructions

1. Season the pork to taste with sea salt and freshly ground black pepper.
2. Melt some cooking fat in a large skillet placed over a high heat and brown the roast on all sides.
3. Using a sharp knife, cut 3-inch deep slits into the pork.
4. Insert the apple slices into each of the pork slits.
5. Place half of the remaining apples in the bottom of an instant pot.
6. Place the roast over the apples.
7. Drizzle the honey on top of the roast, and then add the onion and remaining apples.
8. Add the chicken stock and sprinkle everything with cinnamon.
9. Lock the lid and set on high pressure for about 25 minutes
10. When the timer beeps, naturally release the pressure for 20 minutes
11. Serve and enjoy your dish!

Nutrition Information

Calories: 283.6| Fat: 20.4g | Carbohydrates: 3.7g | Fiber: 0.3g |Protein: 20.0g

Recipe 73: Crusted Lamb with Dijon Mustard

TIME TO PREPARE
7 minutes

COOK TIME
25 Minutes

SERVING
3-4 People

Ingredients

- 2 racks of lamb
- 1 tbsp of olive oil
- 1 pinch of salt
- 1 pinch of ground black pepper
- 1 cup of fresh leaves of parsley
- 2 minced garlic cloves.
- 1 orange grated zest
- ¾ cup of toasted and finely chopped pecan nuts
- 2 tablespoons of Dijon mustard

Instructions

1. Preheat your Instant Pot by pressing the setting "sauté"
2. Rub the lamb with olive oil
3. Season the lamb with the salt, olive oil and pepper.
4. Arrange your lamb in your Instant Pot.
5. Set the timer to 15 minutes and the pressure to High
6. Meanwhile, combine the garlic, the parsley, the orange zest and the pecan nuts all in a deep bowl.
7. Remove the racks of the lamb of your Instant Pot; then spread on each lamb rack 1tbsp of Dijon mustard, herbs and nuts.
8. Divide the mixture between the racks of the lamb evenly
9. Return the lamb to the Instant Pot and keep cooking for about 10 additional minutes.
10. Serve and enjoy your dish with a salad of your choice!

Nutrition Information

Calories: 228| Fat: 11.5g | Carbohydrates: 2.2g | Fiber: 1.2g |Protein: 24.7g

Recipe 74: Instant Pot Lamb Shank

TIME TO PREPARE
5 minutes

COOK TIME
45 Minutes

SERVING
4 People

Ingredients

- 2 lambs shanks of about 1 pound each
- 1 Pinch of salt and 1 pinch of pepper
- 2 Tablespoon of olive oil
- 1 Sliced carrot
- 2 Sliced celery stalks
- 1 Diced onion
- 2 Finely minced garlic cloves
- 3/4 cup of red wine
- 3/4 cup of water
- 4 to 5 peppercorns
- 1 teaspoon of salt
- 2 Rosemary springs
- 2 Tablespoons of cornstarch
- 2 Tablespoons of cold water

Instructions

1. Start by browning the lamb shanks in your Instant Pot by pressing the setting sauté and brown all the sides into olive oil
2. Set your Instant Pot to sauté and sauté the carrots, the celery and the onion into the olive oil for about 3 minutes
3. Add in the garlic and turn off your Instant Pot
4. Deglaze your Instant Pot by adding the wine and the water and scrape the bottom of your Instant Pot with a wooden spoon
5. Add in the peppercorns, the salt and the rosemary and stir very well; then put the meaty ends into the liquid
6. Cover your Instant Pot with the lid and check the sealing ring and make sure the valve is in sealed position
7. Set on manual on High pressure for about 45 minutes
8. Once the pressure cooking time is done; naturally release the pressure for about 10 minutes; then release any remaining pressure manually
9. Remove the meat shanks out of the liquid; then

      combine the cornstarch with the cold water
10. Combine the mixture into your Instant Pot and set it on the function sauté; then cook while stirring for about 5 minutes to thicken your gravy!

Nutrition Information

Calories: 832| Fat: 45g | Carbohydrates: 23g | Fiber: 4g |Protein: 66g

Recipe 75: Lamb Kheema

TIME TO PREPARE
6 minutes

COOK TIME
10 Minutes

SERVING
4 People

Ingredients

- 1 tablespoon of vegetable oil
- 3 to 4 sticks of Indian cinnamon stick; broken into small pieces
- 4 to 5 Cardamom pods
- 1 Cup of chopped yellow onions
- 1 tbsp of minced Garlic
- 1 tbsp of minced fresh ginger
- 1 lb of ground lamb
- 1 tsp of garam masala
- 1 tsp of salt
- 1/2 tsp of ground turmeric
- 1/2 tsp of cayenne

Instructions

1. Start the Instant Pot by pressing the setting sauté; then add in the ghee when the oil is hot
2. Add in the cinnamon sticks and the cardamom pods and sizzle for about 10 seconds
3. Add in the onions, the garlic and the ginger and cook while stirring for about 1 to 2 minutes
4. Add in the lamb; the Garam Masala, the salt, the turmeric, the cayenne, the coriander, the cumin and the water and select the "cancel" button
5. Lock the lid of your Instant Pot and close the valve; then select "MANUAL" and set your Instant Pot to High pressure for about 10 minutes
6. When the pressure cooking time ends up; allow the instant pot to set aside for about 10 minutes; then release any remaining pressure
7. Add in the peas and cover for about 5 minutes
8. Serve and enjoy your dish!

- pepper
- 1/2 tsp of ground coriander
- 1/2 tsp of ground cumin
- 1/4 cup of water
- 1 cup of frozen peas, thawed

Nutrition Information

Calories: 290| Fat: 16.81g | Carbohydrates: 16.69g | Fiber: 3.6g |Protein: 19.65g

Recipe 76: Instant Pot Lamb meatballs with olive sauce

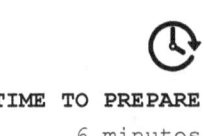

TIME TO PREPARE
6 minutes

COOK TIME
16 Minutes

SERVING
4 People

Ingredients

- 1 1/2 pounds of ground lamb
- 1 Beaten egg
- 1/2 cup of breadcrumbs
- 1/2 cup of feta cheese crumbled, plus extra for garnish
- 2 tablespoons of parsley finely chopped, plus extra for garnish
- 1 tablespoon of finely chopped mint
- 1 tablespoon of Water
- 4 finely minced garlic cloves
- 1/2 teaspoon of kosher salt plus more for the sauce
- 1/4 teaspoon of black pepper plus more for

Instructions

1. Clean the lamb chops and pat it dry with clean paper towels
2. Season the lamb with a combination of parsley, oregano, onion powder
3. Rub the mixture over the lamb chops; then squeeze the lemon juice over the top
4. Sear the lamb chops; then set your Instant Pot to the sauté function and add in the olive oil
5. Squeeze the lemon juice on top of the lamb chops and sear the lamb by sautéing the lamb chops by pressing the sautéing
6. Sear the lamb chop by pressing the function sauté; then add in the olive oil
7. When the olive oil is heated; add in the lamb chops and sear for about 2 minutes without moving the lamb; then sear the other side without moving it; then turn and sear on the other side for 2 additional minutes
8. Pour in 1 cup of water in the inner pot of your Instant Pot; then scrape the inner pot of your Instant Pot and scrape to deglaze it
9. Place the trivet in the inner pot of your Instant pot

- the sauce
- 2 tablespoons of extra-virgin olive oil
- 1 Finely chopped onion
- 1 Finely chopped bell pepper
- 28 ounces of crushed tomatoes juice. About 1 can
- 6 ounces of tomato sauce; 1 can
- 1 teaspoon of dried oregano
- 1/3 cup of pitted and chopped Kalamata olives

10. Place the seared lamb chops on the trivet; then cover with the lid and put the vent in sealing position
11. Set your Instant Pot to pressure cooker at high for about 6 minutes
12. Do a 5 minutes natural release and once the Instant Pot is depressurized; open the lid and take out the lamb chops; then set aside to rest for about 5 minutes
13. Serve and enjoy your dish!

Nutrition Information

Calories: 334.0| Fat: 20.7g | Carbohydrates: 21.7g | Fiber: 13.6g |Protein: 17.4g

Recipe 77: Instant Pot Cheddar Cheese Sandwich

TIME TO PREPARE
10 minutes

COOK TIME
60 Minutes

SERVING
3-4 People

Ingredients

- 2 lbs of beef chuck roast
- 1 Package of dry onion soup
- 2 cups of beef broth
- 1 1/2 cups of shredded sharp cheddar
- 6 sandwich buns

Instructions

1. Start by cutting the meat roast into half; then place in your Instant Pot and sprinkle the onion soup on the top
2. Pour in the broth; then cover your Instant Pot and secure the lid very well
3. Make sure that the valve is in sealed position and set the manual pressure cook button to about 60 minutes
4. Let the pressure naturally release for about 20 minutes; then move the valve to venting to remove any pressure
5. Remove the lid of your Instant Pot; then place the beef over a cutting board and return the shredded meat to the juices in the Instant Pot
6. Toast the buns under the broiler; then pile the beef over the top with about 1/4 cup of cheddar cheese for about 1 minute
7. Serve and enjoy your dish!

Nutrition Information

Calories: 384| Fat: 14g | Carbohydrates: 34g | Fiber: 0g |Protein: 12g

Recipe 78: Instant Pot Oxtails

TIME TO PREPARE
6 minutes

COOK TIME
50 Minutes

SERVING
4 People

Ingredients

- 2 Pounds of medium-cut oxtail pieces
- 2 teaspoons of molasses
- 2 teaspoons of kosher salt
- 1 teaspoon of garlic powder
- 1 teaspoon of onion powder
- 1/2 teaspoon of black pepper
- 1/2 teaspoon of paprika
- 2 tablespoons of canola oil
- 1 cup of unsalted

Instructions

1. Put the oxtails in a large bowl; then add in the molasses and sprinkle with the black pepper; the salt; the garlic powder, the onion powder and the paprika
2. Remove the lid from an Instant pot and press the setting sauté; then when the word Hot disppalys; use the "ADJUST" to select the mode "More"
3. When the word "Hot" appears; add in the oil and cook for about 10 minutes
4. Pour in the stock; then add the remaining ingredients and stir
5. Close the lid of your Instant Pot and turn the steam release handle to "sealing" position
6. Press the [Manual]; and select "High Pressure", and use the buttons [-] or [+] to choose about 50 minutes as pressure cooking time.
7. When the time is up, turn off the Instant Pot; then carefully the release
8. Discard the thyme sprigs and the bay leaf.

- chicken stock
- 4 Finely minced garlic cloves
- 1 large, finely chopped white onion
- 3 finely chopped green onions
- 3 Fresh thyme sprigs
- 3 tablespoons of tomato paste
- 1 medium chopped tomato
- 1 bay leaf
- 1 can of about 15.5 oz of cannellini beans
- 1/4 teaspoon of crushed red pepper

9. Add in more salt to taste; then serve the oxtails with gravy over warm rice, or any other starch of your choice
10. Enjoy your dish!

Nutrition Information

Calories: 350.9| Fat: 19.2g | Carbohydrates: 12| Fiber: 0.0g |Protein: 41.4g

Recipe 79: Beef Koftas

TIME TO PREPARE
5 minutes

COOK TIME
16 Minutes

SERVING
6-7 People

Ingredients

- 2 lb of lean ground beef
- 4 tbsp of minced ginger
- 4 Finely minced garlic cloves
- 4 tbsp of vegetable oil
- 2 Large egg yolks
- 2 tbsp of corn starch
- 1 tsp of salt
- 1 tsp of turmeric
- 1/2 tsp of ground coriander

Instructions

1. In a large bowl; add the ginger, the garlic, the oil, the egg yolk, the cornstarch and the spices.
2. Stir very well; then add in the beef and blend very well
3. Divide the mixture into about 16 portions and shape each into a small ball
4. Put the meatballs in your Instant Pot and select the function "sauté"
5. Press the button "Cancel" and close the lid of your Instant Pot
6. Set the timer for about 16 minutes and the pressure to HIGH
7. Quickly release the pressure through the steam vent
8. When it is safe to open the lid; open it; open it
9. Serve and enjoy your dish!

Nutrition Information

Calories: 237| Fat: 11.22g | Carbohydrates: 7.93| Fiber: 2g |Protein: 25.8g

Recipe 80: Beef Vindaloo

TIME TO PREPARE
10 minutes

COOK TIME
50 Minutes

SERVING
7 People

Ingredients

- 1 Pound of Beef, chopped into chunks of 3cm each
- 1 Medium onion, chopped into wedges
- 2 Sliced Green Chile
- 2 Roughly chopped tomatoes
- 150 ml of Water
- 2 Tbsp of Ghee

For the Marinade:

- 1/2 Tsp of Ground Cinnamon
- 1/4 Tsp of Ground Cloves
- 1 Tsp of Armchoor, AKA mango powder
- 1 Tsp of Ground Turmeric

Instructions

1. Add all of the ingredients for the marinade, except for the cardamom pods to a blender and blitz to a paste
2. Add the obtained paste with the cardamom pods to the diced beef and let marinade for about 12 hours
3. When the marinade is finished up; heat the ghee in your Instant Pot on High on the sauté mode
4. Sauté for about 10 minutes; add in the beef with the marinade for about 5 minutes
5. Add the rest of the ingredients to your Instant Pot; then seal the lid and cook for about 35 minutes on high pressure with about 10 minutes of natural pressure release.
6. When the pressure has been completely released; remove the solid bits from the sauce with a spoon and let sauté on high for about 10 minutes
7. Return the beef meat to the sauce and stir very well
8. Serve and enjoy your dish!

- 1/2 Tsp of Ground Cumin
- 2 Tbsp of Kashmiri Chili Powder
- 1/2 Tsp of Ground Black Pepper
- 1/4 finely chopped Onion
- 8 Minced garlic Cloves Garlic
- 25 g Ginger
- 1 Tbsp Lemon Juice
- 1 Tsp Coarse Sea Salt
- 1 Tsp Honey
- 50 ml Tamarind Pulp
- 3 Tbsp of White Vinegar
- 12 Cardamom Pods, smashed

Nutrition Information

Calories: 237| Fat: 11.22g | Carbohydrates: 7.93| Fiber: 2g |Protein: 25.8g

Recipe 81: Instant Pot Bhuna

TIME TO PREPARE
7 minutes

COOK TIME
15 Minutes

SERVING
5 People

Ingredients

- 2 Tablespoons of vegetable oil for sautéing
- 2 Chopped large onions
- 2 to 3 bay leaves
- 1.5 teaspoons of Ginger-Garlic paste
- 1 1/2 lbs of lamb chunks
- 3/4 teaspoon of cumin powder
- ½ teaspoon of red chilli powder use Kashmiri chilli powder or of paprika powder
- ½ teaspoon of garam

Instructions

1. Turn your Instant pot to "sauté" mode in the "more" setting
2. Add in the vegetable oil; then add in the red onions and the bay leaves
3. Sauté your ingredients until the onions become translucent.
4. Add in the ginger-garlic past; then lamb cubes and the spices including the coriander, the Garam Masala, the cumin, the coriander, the fennel and the red chili powder and stir
5. Add in the canned tomatoes and stir with the remaining ingredients and make sure to scrape any bits of onion or of ginger garlic paste that may stick
6. Add in the salt and stir to combine
7. Cover your Instant Pot with the lid and place the valve in "sealing" position
8. Set the timer for about 5 minutes; then pressure cook and let the steam naturally release
9. Let the valve release the steam for about 10 minutes; then life the vent so that you release any

- masala
- ½ teaspoon of coriander powder
- 3/4 teaspoon of fennel powder
- 1.5 cups of canned chopped tomatoes
- 1 Pinch of salt

remaining pressure
10. Serve and enjoy your dish!

Nutrition Information

Calories: 415| Fat: 23g | Carbohydrates: 14| Fiber: 4g |Protein: 39g

Recipe 82: Instant Pot Lamb Sausage

TIME TO PREPARE
4 minutes

COOK TIME
20 Minutes

SERVING
3-4 People

Ingredients

- 2 Packages of 19 oz of Italian Sweet Sausages
- 4 Finely sliced peppers
- 4 Finely sliced green peppers
- 1 large sliced onion
- 1 tbsp of Italian seasoning
- 2 teaspoon of minced garlic
- 1 can of tomato sauce
- 1 cup of chicken broth

Instructions

1. Combine your ingredients in your Instant pot.
2. Close the lid and set the valve to sealing position
3. Set the pressure to High and the timer to about 20 minutes
4. When the pressure cooking is finished; do a quick release method to remove any pressure
5. Slice the sausage
6. Serve and enjoy your dish!

Nutrition Information

Calories: 711| Fat: 59g | Carbohydrates: 12| Fiber: 3g |Protein: 29g

Recipe 83: Shepherd's Pie

TIME TO PREPARE
5 minutes

COOK TIME
20 Minutes

SERVING
4 People

Ingredients

For the Meat layer
- 1 pound of extra lean ground beef
- 1/2 finely chopped medium onion
- 2 Finely minced garlic cloves
- 2 Teaspoons of tomato paste
- 1 teaspoon of Worcestershire sauce
- 1/2 teaspoon of salt
- 1 teaspoon of onion powder
- 1 teaspoon of garlic powder
- 1 teaspoon of dried oregano
- 1/2 teaspoon of pepper
- 1/2 teaspoon of paprika
- 3 tablespoons of cornstarch
- 1 cup of frozen

Instructions

1. Preheat your oven to about 375°F.
2. Mix all your ingredients for the meat layer in one a stackable pans
3. Mix all your ingredients for the potatoes layer in another stackable pan and cover with a lid
4. Secure both the pans; then add 2 cups of water to the Instant Pot
5. Place the pans ion your Instant Pot and close the lid
6. Turn the valve to sealing position
7. Press the Manual or the Pressure Cooker button to select 20 minutes
8. Once the pressure cooking timer beeps, do a quick release method for about 2 minutes
9. Carefully open your Instant Pot; then remove any stackable inserts
10. Carefully open your Instant Pot; then remove the stackable pans
11. Mash the potatoes without draining it; then lightly mix the meat with a fork
12. Cover the meat with the mashed potatoes and smooth the top
13. Place your pan in the oven and bake for about 20 minutes; then broil for about 3 minutes
14. Let your dish cool; then serve and enjoy your dish!

vegetables
- 1/4 cup of water

For the Mashed Potatoes layer:
- 1.5 pounds of peeled chopped potatoes
- 1 tablespoon of butter, chopped into pieces
- 1/2 cup of broth
- 1/2 cup of milk
- 1 Pinch of salt and 1 pinch of pepper

Nutrition Information

Calories: 272| Fat: 8.21g | Carbohydrates: 34.46| Fiber: 3.4g |Protein: 15.55g

Recipe 84: Instant Pot Swiss steak

TIME TO PREPARE
4 minutes

COOK TIME
20 Minutes

SERVING
3People

Ingredients

- 1 and 1/2 pounds of beef round steak, chopped into 6 pieces
- 1/2 teaspoon of salt
- 1/4 teaspoon of pepper
- 1 Medium, finely chopped onion into slices of about ¼ inch each
- 1 Sliced celery
- 2 Cans of about 8 ounces each of tomato sauce

Instructions

1. Sprinkle the steak with 1 pinch of salt and 1 pinch of pepper
2. Place the onion in your Instant Pot; then top with the celery, the tomato sauce and the steak
3. Lock the lid of your Instant Pot and close the pressure release valve
4. Adjust to pressure cook on High pressure for about 20 minutes.
5. Let the pressure release naturally for about 5 minutes; then quick-release any remaining pressure
6. Serve and enjoy your dish!

Nutrition Information

Calories: 257.5| Fat: 12.2g | Carbohydrates: 6.2g| Fiber: 1.3g |Protein: 15.55g

Recipe 85: Instant Pot Leg of lamb with vegetables

TIME TO PREPARE
8 minutes

COOK TIME
25 Minutes

SERVING
6 People

Ingredients

For the Lamb
- 3 to 4 pounds boneless leg of lamb
- 2 to 3 large carrots
- 1 large, finely chopped onion
- 4 Finely minced garlic cloves
- 2 tablespoons of olive oil
- 1 and 1/2 teaspoons of kosher salt
- 1/2 teaspoon of black pepper
- 1 tablespoon of fresh rosemary, finely chopped
- 1 tablespoon of fresh chopped thyme
- 1 and 1/2 cups of chicken stock

For the Sauce:
- 3 tablespoons of cornstarch
- 3 tablespoons of cold water

Instructions

1. Place your ingredients for the leg of the lamb in your Instant Pot
2. Pat the lamb dry with clean paper towels; then tie the lamb meat with a kitchen twine in several places for about 2 inches between the ties
3. Peel the onion and the carrots; then cut the onion into about 6 to 8 wedges
4. Combine all together the garlic with 1 tablespoon of olive oil; the salt, the pepper and the chopped herbs; then rub the mixture over the lamb meat
5. Add in the remaining 1 tablespoon of olive oil to your Instant Pot; then press the setting sauté and when the oil heats up; add in the lamb, and cook for about 8 minutes; make sure to brown all the sides
6. Cancel the function sauté; then add in the sliced carrots and the onion wedges to the Instant pot together with the chicken stock
7. Lock the lid of your Instant Pot into place and make sure to turn the venting knob to the sealing position; then select the manual setting at High pressure and set the timer to about 25 minutes
8. When the time is up; let the pressure naturally release for about 15 minutes
9. Turn the knob to the venting position; then release any remaining pressure

10. Drain the liquids to a large bowl; then discard the fats and return the liquids to the Instant Pot and press the setting function sauté
11. Mix 3 tablespoons of cornstarch with ¼ cup of cold water and mix until your get a smooth mixture and the mixture starts thickening
12. Adjust the taste with salt and pepper; then serve and enjoy your dish with vegetables!

Nutrition Information

Calories: 219| Fat: 14g | Carbohydrates: 6.2g| Fiber: 1.3g |Protein: 22g

CHAPTER 7: TURKEY, GOOSE AND DUCK RECIPES

Recipe 86: Instant Pot Goose

TIME TO PREPARE
8 minutes

COOK TIME
25 Minutes

SERVING
3-4 People

Ingredients

- 2 tbsp of olive oil
- 2 1/2 lb of wild goose breast
- 4 oz of sliced mushrooms
- 1 medium, finely chopped yellow onion
- 2 cups of beef broth
- 1 1/2 cups of almond milk
- 2 tbsp of corn starch
- 2 tbsp of red wine vinegar
- 1 tbsp of paprika
- 2 tbsp of gluten free soy sauce
- 1 tsp of pepper
- 1/2 tsp of salt

Instructions

1. Add in 2 tbsp of olive oil to your Instant Pot.
2. Turn on your Instant Pot to the sauté function; and when it gets hot, add in the goose hearts and sear it on both sides
3. Remove the goose beasts from you Instant Pot and add in the sliced mushrooms and the chopped onion
4. Cook until the onion start softening up
5. Pour in the 2 cups of beef broth to your Instant Pot; then deglaze to remove any brown bits from the bottom
6. Pour in the almond milk, the red wine vinegar, the gluten free soy sauce, the corn starch, the paprika, the salt and the pepper; then stir to combine very well
7. Cover your Instant Pot with a lid and turn the steam release handle to sealing position and set your Instant Pot to High pressure for about 18 minutes
8. When the pressure cooking time is finished, do a natural release for about 8 minutes
9. Carefully remove the goose breast from the Instant Pot and turn on the sauté function
10. Thicken the sauce; then slice the goose breasts in a

thin way
11. Serve and enjoy your dish

Nutrition Information

Calories: 202| Fat: 10.78g | Carbohydrates: 12g| Fiber: 2g |Protein: 24.6g

Recipe 87: Goose Barbacoa

TIME TO PREPARE
5 minutes

COOK TIME
90 Minutes

SERVING
4 People

Ingredients

- 3½ pounds of goose legs and breasts
- 1 Finely sliced red onion
- 6 Smashed and roughly garlic cloves
- ¼ Cup of apple Cider Vinegar
- 2 Juiced Limes
- 1 Tablespoon of fish sauce
- 4 Roughly chopped peaches
- 2 cans of chili into adobo
- ½ Qt of beef stock
- 1 teaspoon of cumin
- 2 teaspoon of oregano
- 1.2 teaspoons of cloves
- 1.2 teaspoons of paprika

Instructions

1. Heat a large Instant Pot over a medium High heat; then add in 2 tablespoons of oil and once the oil heats up; brown the pieces of meat on each of the sides
2. Remove each piece of meat to a separate pan; then add 2 tablespoon of oil and the red onion
3. Brown the onion for a couple of minutes
4. Add in the garlic and cook for about 1 minute; then add the rest of the ingredients; the peaches, the fish sauce, the ACV, the Lime Juice, the Beef Stock, the Spices, and the Chilies in the Adobo Sauce; then return the browned meat to the Instant pot and stir very well
5. Lock the lid of the Instant Pot into place and pressure cook for about 90 minutes
6. When the meat starts to fall apart, remove the pieces out of the sauce; then shred the meat with forks and reserve the sauce to baste the meat in it
7. Serve and enjoy your dish!

- 1 cinnamon stick
- Oil for Browning

Nutrition Information

Calories: 199| Fat: 9g | Carbohydrates: 6g| Fiber: 0g |Protein: 21g

Recipe 88: Duck Confit

TIME TO PREPARE
6 minutes

COOK TIME
30 Minutes

SERVING
3 People

Ingredients

- 4 to 5 duck legs
- 1 teaspoon of fine sea salt
- ½ teaspoon of Herbes de Provence
- 1 tablespoon of vegetable oil

Instructions

1. Season the duck legs: Sprinkle the duck legs evenly with the salt and the Herbes de Provence.
2. Pour in 1 cup of water into your Instant Pot, pressure cooker; then place the pressure cooker rack in your Instant Pot, and then put a pressure cooker rack into the pot. Put the duck legs on the rack in a loose pile.
3. Pressure cook the duck legs for 30 minutes
4. Do a quick release pressure method; then press the setting sauté and brown the duck legs with the side down for about 3 minutes
5. Flip the duck legs and brown on the other side for about 2 additional minutes; then serve and enjoy your dish!

Nutrition Information

Calories: 215| Fat: 12.2g | Carbohydrates: 0.1g| Fiber: 2g |Protein: 24.6g

Recipe 89: Honey Glazed Turkey wings

TIME TO PREPARE
8 minutes

COOK TIME
20 Minutes

SERVING
4 People

Ingredients

- 3 Minced garlic cloves of garlic
- 1/3 cup of red wine vinegar
- ¼ cup of hot honey with some crushed red pepper
- ½ Cup of spicy duck sauce
- ¼ Cup of Frank's Red Hot
- 2 tablespoons of BBQ sauce
- 2 teaspoons of soy sauce
- 3 tablespoons of olive oil
- 1 package of turkey wings, chopped into pieces
- Salt, pepper, granulated garlic
- Chopped fresh parsley

Instructions

1. In a small bowl, combine all of the ingredients for the sauce; then whisk very well and set aside
2. Season the turkey wings with the salt, the pepper; the granulated garlic and mix very well with your clean hands
3. Put the ingredients in your Instant Pot; then add in the sauce and mix very well with your hands
4. Close the lid of your Instant Pot and lock into place; make sure the steam valve is in sealed position
5. Set the timer for about 8 to 10 minutes; in the meantime, heat up the BBQ sauce
6. When the pressure cooking cycle ends up; quick release the pressure; then remove the turkey wings from the Instant Pot when it is safe to open it and place over a tin foiled lined baking sheet
7. Turn your pressure cooker to the function sauté and cook for about 3 minutes
8. Turn off your Instant Pot; then spread the sauce all over the turkey wings and broil for several minutes
9. Transfer the turkey wings to a serving platter; then sprinkle with chopped fresh parsley
10. Serve and enjoy your dish!

for garnish, optional

Nutrition Information

Calories: 426| Fat: 23g | Carbohydrates: 0g| Fiber: 0g |Protein: 51g

Recipe 90: Instant Pot Ragout

TIME TO PREPARE
6 minutes

COOK TIME
10 Minutes

SERVING
3 People

Ingredients

- 1 tablespoon of extra virgin olive oil
- 1 lb of bulk Italian turkey sausage
- 1 large, thinly sliced red onion
- 1 large, cut into half, cored and thinly sliced fennel bulb
- 4 Garlic cloves
- 2 Tablespoons of chopped fresh thyme
- 1 Pinch of salt
- 1 Pinch of freshly ground black pepper
- 1 ½ cups of bone broth or of chicken broth
- ¾ cup of dry vermouth or dry white wine
- ¼ cup of fresh flat-

Instructions

1. Press the setting sauté of your Instant Pot and heat the olive oil in it
2. When the oil heats up; add in the sausage and cook for about 4 to 5 minutes
3. Add in the red onion, the fennel, the garlic, the thyme, the salt, and the pepper and cook while stirring for about 4 minutes
4. Pour in the chicken broth and the white wine
5. Close the lid of your Instant Pot and seal the valve; then set the timer to about 5 minutes
6. When the timer beeps; turn off your Instant Pot and do a quick release pressure
7. When it is safe to do, open your Instant Pot; then transfer to a serving platter and add in the chopped parsley
8. Serve and enjoy your ragout with cheese!

- leaf chopped parsley
- ¼ cup of grated parmigiano-reggiano cheese for garnish
- Cooked quinoa

Nutrition Information

Calories: 481| Fat: 39g | Carbohydrates: 4g| Fiber: 2.2g |Protein: 19g

Recipe 91: Instant pot Duck with Cranberry Sauce

TIME TO PREPARE
5 minutes

COOK TIME
16 Minutes

SERVING
4 People

Ingredients

- 1 ½ tablespoons of butter
- 3 Tablespoons of chopped shallots
- ½ cup of port
- ¼ cup of red currant jelly
- 1 tablespoon of red wine vinegar
- 1 teaspoon of sugar
- 1/4 cup of sweetened dried cranberries
- 3 tablespoons of dried tart cherries
- ¾ teaspoon of salt, divided
- ¼ teaspoon of black pepper, divided
- 2 teaspoons of olive oil
- 4 Boneless and skinless halved duck breasts

Instructions

1. Melt 1 and ½ teaspoons of butter in your Instant Pot by pressing the setting function sauté
2. Add in the shallots and sauté for about 1 minute; then add the port, the jelly, the vinegar, and the sugar; and cook for about 2 minutes or until the sugar dissolves.
3. Stir in the cranberries and the cherries and cook for about 2 minutes
4. Add in the butter and ¼ teaspoon of salt as well as 1/8 teaspoon of pepper
5. Close the lid of your Instant Pot and set the timer for about 5 to 7 minutes and make sure the valve is in sealed position
6. While your sauce is cooking; heat the oil in a medium non-stick skillet over a medium high heat; then sprinkle with the ½ teaspoon of salt and ½ teaspoon of pepper; then add the duck to the pan
7. Add in the remaining 1/8 teaspoon of pepper; then when the pressure cooking cycle ends up, transfer the duck to the skillet and cook for about 4 minutes per side
8. Serve and enjoy your dish with sauce!

Nutrition Information

Calories: 740| Fat: 43g | Carbohydrates: 62g| Fiber: 9g |Protein: 35g

Recipe 92: Duck Tajine

TIME TO PREPARE
5 minutes

COOK TIME
20 Minutes

SERVING
3-4 People

Ingredients

- 4 pieces of duck
- 10 to 11 plums
- 1 tsp of turmeric
- ½ tsp of ginger
- ½ teaspoon of cumin
- 2 tsp of coriander
- 2 tsp of raz el hanout
- 1 tsp of honey
- 100 ml of orange juice
- 100 ml of water
- 1 Pinch of salt
- 1 Pinch of pepper

Instructions

1. Start your electric pressure cooker by pressing the setting sauté
2. Brown the duck in the Instant pot with the skin side down
3. Add in the chopped onions and the duck fat as well as the spices; the orange juice and the water
4. Place the duck pieces back in the Instant Pot and pressure cook for about 15 minutes
5. When the pressure cooking cycle ends; add in the plums and cook for about 5 minutes
6. Serve and enjoy your dish!

Nutrition Information

Calories: 231| Fat: 12g | Carbohydrates: 16g| Fiber: 0g |Protein: 14g

Recipe 93: Instant Pot Duck with walnuts and pomegranate

TIME TO PREPARE
10 minutes

COOK TIME
30 Minutes

SERVING
4 People

Ingredients

- 2 cups of toasted walnuts
- 3 Tablespoons of butter or olive oil, divided
- 2 Finely chopped onions
- 1/3 cup of pomegranate molasses
- ½ cup of chicken stock
- 2 Tablespoons of lemon juice
- 1 and ½ teaspoons of cinnamon
- 1 teaspoon of turmeric
- 2 Tablespoons of brown sugar
- 1 teapsoon of kosher salt
- 1/2 teaspoon of

Instructions

1. Start by placing the toasted walnuts in a food processor; then set it aside
2. Sauté the onions in 2 tablespoons of butter or in olive oil for about 5 minutes in your Instant Pot by pressing the setting sauté
3. Add in the toasted walnuts and cook for about 2 or 3 additional minutes and stir
4. Add in the pomegranate molasses, the chicken stock and the lemon juice and stir
5. Remove the mixture from the heat; then place in a bowl and set aside
6. In a medium bowl; mix the cinnamon with the turmeric; the brown sugar, the salt and the pepper and coat each piece of duck and into the spice mixture
7. Add 1 tablespoon of butter or olive oil to the Instant Pot and press the setting sauté
8. Brown the duck on both sides; the top with the onion and the walnut sauce and pressure cook on High for about 20 minutes
9. Do a quick pressure release method; then when safe

- ground pepper
- 8 bone-in, skin-on duck thighs
- 10 whole peeled garlic cloves
- 3 stems of fresh rosemary
- 4 Finely chopped carrots
- 1 cup of pomegranate seeds

1/2 cup of chopped parsley

to do, open your Instant Pot and garnish with pomegranate seeds and chopped parsley
10. Serve and enjoy your dish!

Nutrition Information

Calories: 557| Fat: 34g | Carbohydrates: 14g| Fiber: 3g |Protein: 50g

Recipe 94: Duck Chili

TIME TO PREPARE
10 minutes

COOK TIME
35 Minutes

SERVING
3-4 People

Ingredients

- 1.5 lbs of duck breast
- 1 teaspoon of salt
- 1 Cup of finely chopped white onions
- 5 Finely minced large garlic cloves garlic
- 1 Large can of fire roasted diced tomatoes
- 1 can of rinsed and drained kidney beans
- 1 Can of 16 oz of rinsed and drained northern beans
- 6 oz of tomato paste
- 12 ounces of brown ale
- 1 tablespoon of Worcestershire sauce
- 1 tablespoon of dried oregano
- 2 teaspoons of ground cumin
- 2 tablespoons of chili powder
- 1 teaspoon of ground

Instructions

1. Start by scoring the fats of the duck breast; then sprinkle with the salt; then place inside the Instant Pot
2. Turn your Instant Pot by pressing the setting sauté
3. Place the duck breast with the fat side down and sear the duck and the onions for about 5 minutes
4. Add in the
5. Remove the duck; then add in the onions and cook for about 5 minutes
6. Add in the duck with the remaining ingredients
7. Turn your Instant Pot on and cook for about 30 minutes; then let the pressure release naturally and when it is safe to do it, open your Instant Pot
8. Remove the duck from your Instant Pot, then shred the meat with a fork
9. Serve and enjoy with garnish of your choice!

black pepper
- 1 teaspoon of Smoked Paprika
- 1 teaspoon of onion powder
- 1 teaspoon of red pepper flakes
- ½ teaspoon of cayenne pepper
- For the Garnishes:

½ cup of chopped cilantro

1 cup of grated parmesan or mozzarella cheese

Nutrition Information

Calories: 850| Fat: 52g | Carbohydrates: 29g| Fiber: 0g |Protein: 63g

Recipe 95: Duck Curry

TIME TO PREPARE
7 minutes

COOK TIME
18 Minutes

SERVING
3 People

Ingredients

- ½ Finely sliced small onion
- 5 to 6 Crimini mushrooms, quartered
- 1 Sliced medium carrot
- 1 Large Chinese or Japanese, chopped eggplant
- 2 to 3 tbsp of curry paste
- ½ Chinese-style roast duck, chopped bone in
- 1 Can of coconut milk, 14 Oz of coconut milk
- 1 chopped zucchini, 1.5 inch chunks
- ½ Sliced bell pepper
- 2 tbsp of fish sauce
- 2 tsp of brown sugar

Instructions

1. Turn on your Instant Pot to Sauté; then drizzle the oil; then add the onion and the mushroom with 1 pinch of salt
2. Sauté for about 1 minute
3. Add the duck, the carrot; the eggplant and the coconut milk, then mix and turn off the sauté function
4. Cook on High pressure for about 4 minutes
5. Naturally release for about 10 minutes; then release the remaining pressure and remove the lid
6. Turn on the sauté function, then add in the bell pepper, the zucchini, the fish sauce and the brown sugar and let simmer for about 2 to 3 minutes
7. Adjust the seasoning to taste; then serve and enjoy your delicious dish!

Nutrition Information

Calories: 446| Fat: 33.4g | Carbohydrates: 13.3g| Fiber: 2.9g |Protein: 21.3g

CHAPTER 8: STOCKS AND SAUCES RECIPES

Recipe 96: Meat Sauce

TIME TO PREPARE
3 minutes

COOK TIME
10 Minutes

SERVING
3 People

Ingredients

- 1/2 large, chopped purple onion
- 1-1.5 pounds of ground beef
- 1 teaspoon of minced garlic
- 2 cans of 15 ounces of tomato sauce
- ½ tablespoon of dried oregano
- ½ tablespoon of dried basil
- 1 teaspoon of crushed red pepper flakes
- ½ teaspoon of garlic powder
- ½ teaspoon of sea salt
- 1-2 cups of freshly chopped basil

Instructions

1. Preheat your Instant Pot by pressing the setting function sauté on the display panel
2. When the display HOT appears, add in the diced purple onion and sauté this chopped purple onion
3. Add in the minced garlic and combine with the sautéed purple onion
4. Add in the ground beef and the onion mixture to your Instant Pot
5. Crumble the ground beef and sauté it it until it becomes brown
6. Excess any grease from the Instant Pot.
7. Add in the tomato sauce, the oregano, the dried basil, the crushed red pepper flakes, the garlic powder, and the sea salt to the mixture of the beef and let simmer for about 10 minutes
8. Press the button Cancel/Keep Warm and let the meat keep warm for about 10 minutes
9. Scoop the sauce and Sprinkle with fresh basil
10. Serve the sauce over Zucchini noodles and enjoy your dish!

Nutrition Information

Calories: 263.2| Fat: 18.6g | Carbohydrates: 10.6g| Fiber: 3.1g |Protein: 11.8g

Recipe 97: Turkey Stock

TIME TO PREPARE
8 minutes

COOK TIME
50 Minutes

SERVING
10 People

Ingredients

- 1 14 pound turkey carcass with most of the meat removed
- 10 cups of water
- 1 teaspoon of sea salt
- 1 teaspoon of black pepper
- 2 to 3 celery stalks with the leaves

Instructions

1. Place a trivet in your Instant Pot; then place the turkey carcass on the trivet
2. Pour the water into the Instant Pot; then add in the sea salt, the pepper and the celery stalks
3. Place the lid on your Instant Pot and turn the valve to sealing position
4. Pressure cook for about 50 minutes
5. Do a 10-minute release; then do a quick release for the remaining pressure to drop completely
6. Hit the button Cancel to turn off your Instant Pot
7. When the pin drops, open the lid and carefully remove the lid of your Instant Pot and discard the carcass
8. Pour in the stock through the mesh strainer into a bowl; then separate into small container and store in the refrigerator

Nutrition Information

Calories: 28.1| Fat: 0.2g | Carbohydrates: 6.8g| Fiber: 1.4g |Protein: 0.5g

Recipe 98: Onion Stock

TIME TO PREPARE
7 minutes

COOK TIME
50 Minutes

SERVING
5 People

Ingredients

- 3 onions
- 1 tablespoon of olive oil
- 1/4 teaspoon of salt
- A pinch of sugar (optional)
- 1 cup of water or stock

Instructions

1. Thinly slice the onions with a mandolin or with a sharp knife
2. Add 1 tablespoon of olive oil to your Instant Pot insert; then press the sauté function button and adjust the heat to "LOW"
3. Add in the onions; then season with salt, and stir
4. Add 1 pinch of sugar and stir
5. Let the onions cook for a few minutes; then deglaze the insert with water or with stock
6. Seal your Instant Pot and make sure that the release valve is set to "Sealing" position; then press the "Manual" or the "Pressure cook" and set the timer for about 35 minutes
7. When the cooking time ends; release the pressure manually; then transfer to jars and store!

Nutrition Information

Calories: 13| Fat: 1g | Carbohydrates: 0.1g| Fiber: 0g |Protein: 0 g

Recipe 99: Corn Stock

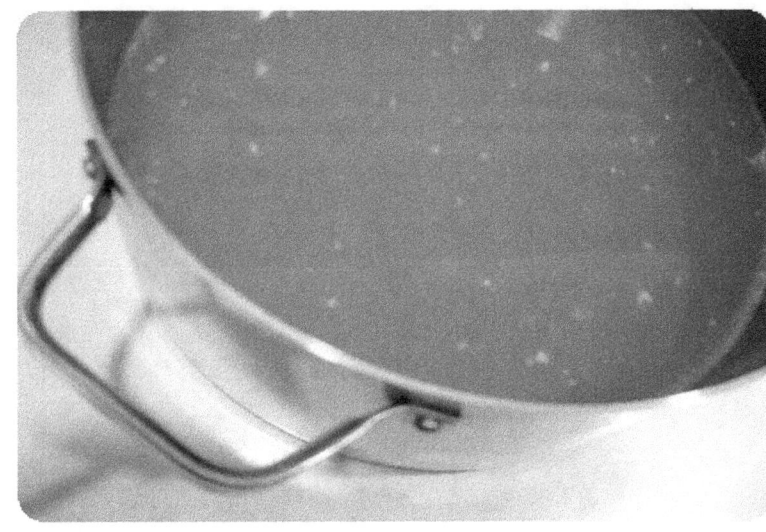

TIME TO PREPARE
7 minutes

COOK TIME
50 Minutes

SERVING
5 People

Ingredients

- 6 to 7 grilled ears of corn
- 1 Quartered onion
- 2 Peeled garlic cloves
- 4 Sprigs of fresh marjoram
- 4 Sprigs of fresh thyme
- 2 to 3 bay leaves
- 2 Pods of star anise
- 12 Whole peppercorns

Instructions

1. Remove kernels from the cobs; then reserve the cobs aside
2. Remove the kernels from the ears
3. Slice the 6 cobs into about three pieces; then add the corn cobs, the remaining seasoning and 8 cups of water to the removable pot of your Instant Pot
4. Close the lid of your Instant Pot and seal the vent.
5. Set the manual High pressure for about 20 minutes; or you can just press the button
6. When the cooking times finishes up; naturally release the pressure for about 15 minutes
7. Use the stock immediately, or store for about 5 days!

Nutrition Information

Calories: 58| Fat: 0.5g | Carbohydrates: 14.1g| Fiber: 1.8g |Protein: 2g

Recipe 100: Shrimp Stock

TIME TO PREPARE
5 minutes

COOK TIME
50 Minutes

SERVING
5 People

Ingredients

- 2 cups of prawns
- 2 large carrots
- 1 Chopped large onion
- 9 garlic cloves
- 1 Celery stalk
- 15 whole peppercorns
- 3 to 4 liters of cold water

Instructions

1. Place all your ingredients in the Instant pot including water up to the 2/3rd
2. Set to the setting "Manual" at high pressure for about 30 minutes.
3. Select the button function "Cancel" and quickly release the pressure
4. Strain the stock; then remove the prawns and the vegetables.
5. Let cool down and chill the stock into the refrigerator!

Nutrition Information

Calories: 76| Fat: 1g | Carbohydrates: 1g| Fiber: 0g |Protein: 15g

Recipe 101: Japanese Stock

TIME TO PREPARE
5 minutes

COOK TIME
10 Minutes

SERVING
6 People

Ingredients

- 1 and 2/3 cups of water
- 1 Konbu of about 2 inch, square
- 2 ½ tablespoons of soy sauce
- 2 tablespoons of mirin
- 1 tablespoon of sake

Instructions

1. Pour the water into an Instant Pot
2. Drop the Konbu into the water and close the lid of your Instant Pot
3. Set the timer to about 5 minutes at High pressure and make sure the valve is in sealed position
4. When the timer beeps, do a quick release pressure; then when it is safe to do, open the lid of yoru Instant Pot
5. Add the soy sauce, the mirin, and the sake and press the setting sauté
6. Cook for about 5 minutes; then remove the Konbu and let it cool completely
7. Pour the stock in a bottle, seal and store it in the refrigerator

Nutrition Information

Calories: 27| Fat: 3.3g | Carbohydrates: 0.7g| Fiber: 0g |Protein: 0g

Recipe 102: Lobster Stock

TIME TO PREPARE
5 minutes

COOK TIME
30 Minutes

SERVING
5 People

Ingredients

- 4 cups of water
- Lobster shells from 2 lbs of lobsters
- ½ Cup of packed parsley
- 1 Sliced celery stick
- 1 Quartered onion
- 2 to 3 small bay leaves

Instructions

1. Add the water to the inner pot of your Instant Pot.
2. Add the lobster shells, the parsley, the celery, the onion and the bay leaves.
3. Stir your ingredients very well to combine.
4. Pressure cook for about 30 minutes
5. When the timer beeps, do a Natural Pressure Release
6. Place a colander in a bowl; then drain the contents of the inner pot in your colander.
7. Transfer the broth to a clean jar or container
8. Store the stock in the refrigerator and store for about 3days

Nutrition Information

Calories: 18.7| Fat: 0.6g | Carbohydrates: 3.2g| Fiber: 0.6g |Protein: 0.5g

Recipe 103: Duck Stock

TIME TO PREPARE
4 minutes

COOK TIME
50 Minutes

SERVING
6 People

Ingredients

- 1 Duck carcass or bones from a roasted duck
- 2 to 3 cups of vegetable scraps carrot peels, Celery, onion, and garlic
- 1 Sprig of thyme
- 1 tablespoon of kosher salt
- 1 teaspoon of peppercorns
- 2 to 3 bay leaves
- 10 cups of cold water

Instructions

1. Place all your ingredients in your Electric pressure cooker and set the valve to sealed position
2. Set the pressure for High and set the timer for about 50 minutes
3. Do a natural release pressure for about 30 minutes.
4. Strain the stock and let cool
5. Store the stock for immediate or later use!

Nutrition Information

Calories: 10| Fat: 0.2g | Carbohydrates: 1g| Fiber: 0.0g |Protein: 2g

Recipe 104: Fish Stock

TIME TO PREPARE
5 minutes

COOK TIME
40 Minutes

SERVING
7-8 People

Ingredients

- 1 to 2 fish tails, heads and collars
- 1 to 2 fish fillets, any type of white fish you like
- 2 to 3 celery ribs
- ½ Finely chopped onion
- 1 to 2 carrots
- 1 tsp of thyme
- 1 Pinch of salt
- 1 Pinch of pepper
- 1 to 2 bay leaves

Instructions

1. Add all your ingredients to the instant pot cooking insert
2. Fill your Instant pot with enough quantity of water to cover the ingredients by an inch or two.
3. Cover your Instant Pot with the lid; then move the toggle switch to sealed position
4. Press the setting manual at high pressure for about 40 minutes
5. After the pressure cooking time ends up, do a quick release method to expel any remaining steam
6. Carefully remove the lid of your Instant Pot
7. With the help of a large bowl and a colander in it, ladle the soup with the ingredients in a colander and sieve the solids from your broth
8. Discard the solids; then pour the broth in secure containers and store in the refrigerator!

Nutrition Information

Calories: 94| Fat: 2g | Carbohydrates: 1g| Fiber: 0 g |Protein: 17g

Recipe 105: Korean-Style Stock

TIME TO PREPARE
6 minutes

COOK TIME
35 Minutes

SERVING
6 People

Ingredients

- 10 cups of Cold water
- 2 Sheets of dried seaweed, palm size Kombu/ Dasima
- 3 to 4 Dried shiitake mushrooms
- 3 Small green onions
- 9 Smashed Garlic Cloves
- 5 Ginger slices of about ¼ inch of thickness
- ½ Roughly chopped large yellow onion
- 1 Tablespoon of Black peppercorns
- 5 Large dried anchovy for sock or ¼ cup of dried Pollack

Instructions

1. Add all your ingredients to your Instant Pot
2. Cover your Instant Pot with the lid and lock it in position
3. Make sure the valve is in sealed position
4. Set the timer to about 30 to 35 minutes and set the pressure to High
5. When the pressure cooking cycle comes to an end; turn the valve to venting and do a quick release method for 15 to 20 minutes
6. Open the lid when it is safe to do; then remove the seaweeds
7. Store the stock in containers; then keep in the refrigerator

Nutrition Information

Calories: 39| Fat: 0g | Carbohydrates: 10g| Fiber: 3 g |Protein: 1g

Recipe 106: Mushroom Broth

TIME TO PREPARE
5 minutes

COOK TIME
13 Minutes

SERVING
5-6 People

Ingredients

- 8 cups of water
- ½ Cup of dried porcini mushrooms
- 6 Medium peeled and smashed garlic cloves of garlic
- 1 Teaspoon of scant
- 1 teaspoon of fine grain sea salt
- ½ teaspoon of freshly ground pepper
- 1 or 2 sprigs of fresh thyme

Instructions

1. Combine the dried mushrooms with the water and the garlic in your Instant pot
2. Close your Instant Pot and turn the Valve to SEAL position
3. Pressure cook on high for about 10 minutes.
4. Carefully quick release; then gently shake or tap your Electric pressure cooker
5. Season with the pepper and the salt as well as the thyme; then wait for 1 to 2 minutes and stir
6. Adjust the taste of salt to your liking
7. Store the broth in the refrigerator for days!

Nutrition Information

Calories: 5| Fat: 0.0g | Carbohydrates: 1g| Fiber: 0.0 g |Protein: 0g

Recipe 107: Fennel and Crab Broth

TIME TO PREPARE
5 minutes

COOK TIME
20 Minutes

SERVING
6 People

Ingredients

- 1 Tablespoon of Olive oil
- 4 cracked crab claws
- 1 Small, finely diced fennel bulb
- 1 Small, finely diced onion
- 1 Finely chopped garlic clove
- 2 Finely diced celery stalks
- ½ Deseeded and chopped red chilli
- 1 Splash of white wine
- 4 to 5 ripe, deseeded and chopped plum tomatoes
- ¼ Pound of picked

Instructions

1. Heat your Instant Pot by pressing the setting sauté
2. Add a splash of oil
3. When display HOT appears; add in the crab claws and sauté for about 7 minutes
4. Add in the fennel, the onion, the garlic, the celery and the chili
5. Add in the wine and pour over 750ml of water; then close the lid of your Instant Pot and seal the valve
6. Set the timer for about 15 minutes and the pressure to HIGH
7. When the pressure cooking times ends; do a quick release pressure; then open the lid when it is safe to do and add in the tomatoes and the crab meat; then season very well
8. Press the setting sauté and cook for about 5 additional minutes
9. Garnish with the fennel fronds; then serve with claw on top
10. Enjoy!

fresh white crab meat
- 1 Handful of small fennel fresh dill
- 1 Pinch of salt and 1 of black pepper

Nutrition Information

Calories: 106| Fat: 7g | Carbohydrates: 10g| Fiber: 3g |Protein: 2g

Recipe 108: Spicy Broth

TIME TO PREPARE
5 minutes

COOK TIME
12 Minutes

SERVING
6 People

Ingredients

- 1 Piece of 2 inch of peeled ginger
- 3 Smashed garlic cloves
- 1 bulb of onion
- 1 Serrano pepper
- 1 stalk of lemongrass
- 9 black peppercorns
- 2 to 3 star anises
- 2 to 3 whole cloves
- 6 cups of water

Instructions

1. Slice the ginger, the bulb onion, the pepper and the lemongrass lengthwise.
2. Place in the Instant Pot pan; then cover with cool water.
3. Turn on your Instant Pot; then click the Manual button and change the time to about 12 minutes.
4. Release the pressure manually.
5. Season with 1 pinch of salt to taste
6. Serve or store your broth!

Nutrition Information

Calories: 33.2| Fat: 0.7g | Carbohydrates: 5.5g| Fiber: 0.2g |Protein: 2g

Recipe 109: Dashi Kombu

TIME TO PREPARE
5 minutes

COOK TIME
20 Minutes

SERVING
5 People

Ingredients

- 1 piece of 4 inches of dashi kombu
- 4 Cups of water

Instructions

1. Start by wiping the Kombu with a damp cloth.
2. Cut into pieces of about 1 inch the Kombu
3. Pour the water in your Instant Pot; then add in the chopped Kombu
4. Lock the lid of the Instant Pot and make sure the valve is in sealed position
5. Set the timer for about 20 minutes and the pressure to High
6. When the timer beeps and the cooking pressure cycle ends up, turn off your Instant pot and do a quick release pressure for about 10 minutes
7. Open the lid when it is safe to do
8. Let cool for a few minutes the broth; then strain through a mesh strainer
9. Store the broth in containers!

Nutrition Information

Calories: 4.3| Fat: 0.1g | Carbohydrates: 1g| Fiber: 0.1g |Protein: 0.2g

Recipe 110: Veggie green stock

TIME TO PREPARE:
8 minutes

COOK TIME
30 Minutes

SERVING
6 People

Ingredients

- 1 Medium, chopped red onion
- 3 Roughly chopped celery stalks
- 1 to 2 roughly chopped carrots
- 2 large garlic cloves
- 1 Inch of ginger
- 1 to 2 bay leaves
- 1 teaspoon of black peppercorn
- 1 teaspoon of dried thyme
- 6 Cups of water
- 1 Pinch of salt, to taste

Instructions

1. Add your ingredients, the onion, the celery, the carrot, the garlic, the ginger, the bay leaf, the black peppercorns and the dried thyme to your Instant Pot
2. Add the salt is using it
3. Pour the water into your Instant Pot; 6 cups of water would be enough
4. Close your Instant Pot with the lid and press the manual button; then cook on High for about 30 minutes
5. When the pressure cooking time ends up; let the pressure naturally release
6. Open the Instant Pot; then strain the stock with a strainer
7. Let cool; then store the stock for a week and use it whenever you need it!

Nutrition Information

Calories: 11| Fat: 0.3g | Carbohydrates: 2g| Fiber: 0.3g |Protein: 0.1g

Recipe 111: Veggie green stock

TIME TO PREPARE:
8 minutes

COOK TIME
30 Minutes

SERVING
6 People

Ingredients

- 1 Medium, chopped red onion
- 3 Roughly chopped celery stalks
- 1 to 2 roughly chopped carrots
- 2 large garlic cloves
- 1 Inch of ginger
- 1 to 2 bay leaves
- 1 teaspoon of black peppercorn
- 1 teaspoon of dried thyme
- 6 Cups of water
- 1 Pinch of salt, to taste

Instructions

8. Add your ingredients, the onion, the celery, the carrot, the garlic, the ginger, the bay leaf, the black peppercorns and the dried thyme to your Instant Pot
9. Add the salt is using it
10. Pour the water into your Instant Pot; 6 cups of water would be enough
11. Close your Instant Pot with the lid and press the manual button; then cook on High for about 30 minutes
12. When the pressure cooking time ends up; let the pressure naturally release
13. Open the Instant Pot; then strain the stock with a strainer
14. Let cool; then store the stock for a week and use it whenever you need it!

Nutrition Information

Calories: 11| Fat: 0.3g | Carbohydrates: 2g| Fiber: 0.3g |Protein: 0.1g

CHAPTER 9: DESSERTS AND BREAD RECIPES

Recipe 112: Brownie Pudding

TIME TO PREPARE: 7 minutes

COOK TIME 30 Minutes

SERVING 4 People

Ingredients

- 1 ½ cups of water
- 7 tablespoons of butter, melted and very well divided
- 1 Cup of sugar
- 2 Large eggs
- ¼ cup of flour
- ¼ cup and 2 tablespoons of unsweetened cocoa powder
- 1 teaspoon of vanilla
- 1/8 teaspoon of salt
- ¼ cup of semisweet chocolate chips
- ¼ cup of milk chocolate chips

Instructions

1. Pour 1 and ½ cups water into your Instant Pot; then place the steam rack in it
2. Butter a baking dish of about 6 to 7 inches with 1 tablespoon of butter
3. In a large bowl, beat all together the eggs and the sugar and beat very well for about 4 to 5 minutes
4. In a small bowl, combine the flour with the cocoa and the salt; then add to the sugar and the eggs mixture
5. Add in the vanilla with the remaining 6 tablespoons of butter and mix
6. Pour the mixture into the prepared dish; then sprinkle with the chocolate
7. Place the dish on the steam rack and secure the lid of your Instant Pot
8. Select the Manual and cook at a high pressure for about 30 minutes
9. Once the pressing cooking time is complete, do a quick release method; then carefully remove the lid
10. Carefully remove the baking dish from the Instant Pot

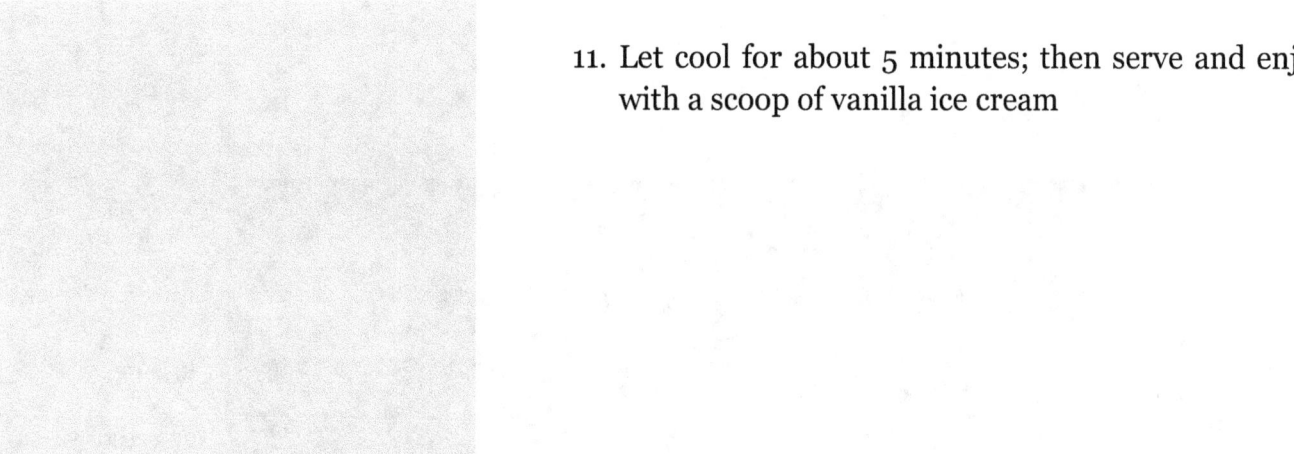

11. Let cool for about 5 minutes; then serve and enjoy with a scoop of vanilla ice cream

Nutrition Information

Calories: 208.8| Fat: 8.5g | Carbohydrates: 37.5g| Fiber: 3.5g |Protein: 5.9g

Recipe 113: Crumbled Apples

TIME TO PREPARE:
5 minutes

COOK TIME
8 Minutes

SERVING
3 People

Ingredients

- 6 Peeled and diced Granny Smith apples
- ¼ Teaspoon of ground nutmeg
- 2 to 2 and ½ teaspoons of finely ground cinnamon
- 2 Tablespoons of maple syrup
- 2 and ½ tablespoons of caramel syrup
- ¼ to ½ Cup of water
- 4 Tablespoons of melted and salted butter
- ¼ Cup of sifted flour
- 1/3 Cup of packed light brown sugar

Instructions

1. Put the apples in your Instant pot
2. Add the nutmeg with the cinnamon, the maple syrup, the caramel sauce and the water
3. Now, make the topping by melting the butter in a heat proof bowl
4. Add the sugar, the flour, the salt and the oats and mix very well
5. Pour the mixture over the apples and lock the lid of the Instant Pot
6. Seal the valve and set the timer of the Instant Pot to about 8 minutes and the pressure to HIGH
7. When the timer beeps, quick release the pressure
8. Serve and enjoy your apples with ice-cream!

- 1 Pinch of sea salt
- ¾ Cup of oats
- Scooped vanilla ice cream for serving

Nutrition Information

Calories: 220| Fat: 6g | Carbohydrates: 40g| Fiber: 7g |Protein: 4g

Recipe 114: Instant Pot chocolate Coated Pears

TIME TO PREPARE:
6 minutes

COOK TIME
5 Minutes

SERVING
3 People

Ingredients

- 1 Halved lemon
- 3 Cups of water
- 2 Cups of white wine
- 2 Cups of organic cane sugar
- 5 Cinnamon sticks
- 6 to 7 Bartlett ripe pears; but make sure it is firm
- To make the chocolate sauce:
- 9 Ounces of bittersweet chocolate cut into pieces
- ½ Cup of coconut milk
- ¼ Cup of coconut oil

Instructions

1. Pour the water, the wine, the sugar and the cinnamon sticks in your Instant Pot and select the function
2. Let your ingredients simmer until your ingredients start dissolving
3. Switch the bottom function to the setting KEEP WARM
4. Peel your pears and rub it with lemon to prevent its color from getting brown
5. Squeeze the remaining quantity of lemon juice to the syrup and wine
6. Place the pears into the syrup and close the lid of your Instant pot, electric pressure cooker
7. Set the timer to about 5 minutes and the pressure to

- 2 Tablespoons of maple syrup

HIGH

8. When the timer beeps; quick release the pressure
9. Remove the pears and set it aside to cool for about 3 minutes
10. Pour the sauce over the pears
11. Now, make your Chocolate Sauce by placing the chocolate into a medium bowl
12. In a separate small saucepan and over a medium flame, heat the milk and the maple syrup; then let boil
13. Pour the mixture over the chocolate and wait for 1 minute
14. When the chocolate becomes smooth, transfer the pears to a serving platter
15. Pour the chocolate sauce over the pears
16. Serve and enjoy your delicious dessert!

Nutrition Information

Calories: 232| Fat: 10.6g | Carbohydrates: 34.2g| Fiber: 6.5g |Protein: 2.2g

Recipe 115: Indian Style Obattu

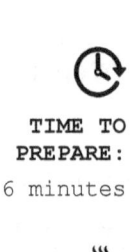

TIME TO PREPARE:
6 minutes

COOK TIME
5 Minutes

SERVING
3 People

Ingredients

- To prepare the dough:
- 2 Cups of whole wheat flour
- ¾ Cup of water
- 3 Teaspoon of ghee
- 1 Pinch of salt
- To prepare the stuffing
- 1 Cup of chana Dal
- 1 and ½ cup of water
- ¼ Teaspoon of cardamom powder
- 1 Cup of jaggery
- 1 Pinch of salt
- ¼ Cup of atta to use it for dusting
- 3 Tbsp of oil or ghee

Instructions

1. In a deep bowl, add the water, the ghee and the salt; then sift in the flour and knead the ingredients very well for 3 minutes.
2. If you see the dough dry, add 2 tbsp of water and knead; then set the dough aside for around 2 hours. Soak your chana Dal in the water for around 1 hour.
3. Cook your soaked chana Dal with around 1 and ½ cup of water in your Instant Pot at high pressure for 5 minutes. When the timer beeps; naturally release the pressure and drain the chana Dal; then grind it with the help of a mixer
4. Add the cardamom powder, the jiggery and the salt.
5. Grind your ingredients until you obtain a very soft paste; add more water while your grind. Then transfer the mixture into a large pan and fry it for around 5 minutes; then set it aside for around 10 minutes.
6. Make around 15 balls out of your mixture and set it

aside above a plate.
7. For the Stuffing of the obbattu: Start by kneading the dough for around 1 minute and make 15 balls of it; then flatten tit with flour.
8. Place 1 ball of the mixture of pooranam lentil into the middle of your dough. Pull up the sides of the dough around your stuffing and pinch it on top to seal it. Repeat the same procedure with the rest of the dough balls.
9. Once you finish, set the balls rest for around 10 minutes. Pat your stuffed balls once again into the flour and then gently roll the dough.
10. If your dough breaks; then add a little bit more of flour and set it aside. And after that, heat 3 tbsp of ghee or vegetable oil in your Instant Pot and press sauté
11. Line the obbattu balls and cook it on each side for 1 to 2 minutes. Finally; serve and enjoy your obbattu

Nutrition Information

Calories: 385| Fat: 10.6g | Carbohydrates: 56g| Fiber: 0g |Protein: 2.2g

Recipe 116: Sweet honey bread

TIME TO PREPARE:
7minutes

COOK TIME
10 Minutes

SERVING
3 People

Ingredients

- 3 Teaspoon of olive oil
- 3 Cups of all purpose flour
- ½ Teaspoon of bicarbonate baking soda
- 1 Teaspoon of salt
- 1 and ¼ cup of whole milk or plain yogurt
- Water
- 3 Tbsp of honey
- 1Tbsp of sugar

Instructions

1. Start by preparing your Instant Pot and place the steaming basket inside it. And grease with oil 4 heat proof containers or a tray that fits the Instant Pot.
2. Meanwhile, combine all together, the flour, the baking soda and the salt, then add the sugar and the honey.
3. Mix the ingredients very well together with the help of a fork and after that; add yogurt, and stir very well and add a little bit of water; then knead the ingredients.
4. Form 4 small dough balls. The sough shall be sticky, but not too much.
5. Place every ball in a container or place all the balls into the baking tray and oil the top or you can brush the top with butter or milk.
6. Cover the containers with foil and make sure they are tightly closed.
7. Lock the lid of the instant pot after lining the containers inside and set at high pressure for 30 minutes.

8. When the timer beeps, naturally release the pressure and let the containers cool for 10 minutes; check with a toothpick and if it comes clean, serve and enjoy your sweet bread!

Nutrition Information

Calories: 100| Fat: 10.6g | Carbohydrates: 56g| Fiber: 0g |Protein: 2.2g

Recipe 117: Whole Wheat Bread

TIME TO PREPARE:
10 minutes

COOK TIME
45 Minutes

SERVING
6 People

Ingredients

- 2 cups of all-purpose flour
- 1 cup of white whole-wheat flour
- 1 ¾ teaspoons of salt
- ½ teaspoon of active dry yeast
- 2 tablespoons plus 1 teaspoon of fresh chopped rosemary
- 1 and ½ cups of room temperature water

Instructions

1. In a large glass bowl large that fits your Instant Pot, mix all together the salt, the flour, the yeast and 2 tablespoons of fresh rosemary.
2. Pour in the water and combine very well with a spatula or a wooden spoon; but don't over mix
3. Place a trivet into the bottom of your Instant Pot, you need to remove the inner cooking pot
4. Cover the bowl with a plastic wrap; then place the trivet in the Instant Pot and turn on the setting function yogurt; then turn the vent to venting
5. Set the timer for about 4 hours for the dough to proof
6. When your dough is done proofing, preheat your oven to 450°F and place a Dutch oven with cover in the oven to warm up
7. Place the dough over a floured counter and shape into a dough
8. Brush the dough with olive oil and sprinkle with sea salt and with the remaining rosemary.
9. Let stand aside; then remove the hot Dutch oven from your oven and uncover it
10. Put the dough ball in your Dutch oven; then cover it

11. Place back in the oven and cook for about 30 minutes
12. Remove the lid and bake for about 15 additional minutes
13. Remove the bread from the oven and let cool before slicing
14. Serve and enjoy your bread!

Nutrition Information

Calories: 133| Fat: 0.6g | Carbohydrates: 27.9g| Fiber: 0.1g |Protein: 4.3g

Recipe 118: Bread with cheese

TIME TO PREPARE:
6 minutes

COOK TIME
10 Minutes

SERVING
4 People

Ingredients

- 1 Italian loaf of bread
- 8 Oz of cream cheese
- 2 Tbsp of unsalted butter
- 1 Teaspoon of garlic powder
- 1 Teaspoon of garlic salt
- 1 Cup of shredded Mozzarella cheese

Instructions

1. Start by preparing your Instant pot and place it over a medium high heat
2. Pour 2 cups of water in the Instant Pot.
3. Place the steaming basket or the trivet in its place in the Instant Pot
4. Meanwhile, slice the Italian loaf of bread into halves lengthwise
5. Place both of the bread halves on a greased baking dish and place an aluminum sling foil in it
6. Spread one thin layer of the butter on both the pieces of your bread.
7. Place the cream cheese and the garlic powder salt all together into a deep bowl and combine it very well.
8. Now spread a layer of the mixture of the cream cheese above the butter and then top it with the shredded Mozzarella cheese

9. Seal the aluminum foil very well from the sides and place the baking dish in your Instant Pot
10. Close the lid and set at high pressure for around 10 minutes.
11. Once the timer beeps, quick release the pressure; then serve and enjoy your cheese bread

Nutrition Information

Calories: 85| Fat: 6.8g | Carbohydrates: 27.9g| Fiber: 0.0g |Protein: 5.1g

Recipe 119: Banana Bread

TIME TO PREPARE:
10 minutes

COOK TIME
50 Minutes

SERVING
6 People

Ingredients

- 2 Cups of low carb baking mix
- 2 to 3 medium, fully ripe and mashed bananas
- 2 Tablespoons of butter room temperature
- 2 Large eggs
- 1/3 Cup of unsweetened apple sauce
- ¼ Cup of sugar
- ¼ Cup of chopped nuts
- 1 and ½ teaspoons of baking soda
- ½ Teaspoon of salt

Instructions

1. Mix the sugar, the softened butter, the unsweetened applesauce and the eggs
2. With a hand mixer, beat your ingredients very well until it becomes smooth
3. Add the unsweetened applesauce and the eggs
4. Beat your mixture very well until it is very well mixed
5. Add in the mashed bananas to your wet ingredients; then fully mix.
6. Add your dry ingredients to your wet ingredients and whisk very well until your ingredients are combined
7. Add in the nuts; then grease a medium loaf baking tray
8. Pour the mixture into the tray; then cover it with an aluminum foil
9. Pour 1 cup of water into your Instant Pot; then place the trivet in its place
10. Put the baking tray over the trivet and make a shape of handle with the aluminum
11. Lock the lid of the Instant Pot and set the timer on the setting Manual for about 50 minutes
12. When the timer beeps; naturally release the pressure after 10 minutes; then remove the baking tray from the Instant Pot

13. Set the bread aside to cool
14. Slice the bread; then serve and enjoy it!

Nutrition Information

Calories: 247| Fat: 8.8g | Carbohydrates: 39g| Fiber: 1.7g |Protein: 3.8g

Recipe 120: Pumpkin Bread

TIME TO PREPARE:
10 minutes

COOK TIME
50 Minutes

SERVING
7 People

Ingredients

- 215g of wheat flour
- 30g of sugar
- 100g of warm fresh milk
- 30g of butter
- 1/3 of an egg
- 1 tbsp of yeast
- 1/2 tbsp of salt

Instructions

1. Combine your ingredients all together except for the butter. Keep mixing your components on a hard surface like marble and use the palms of your hand to make it smooth.
2. Add the butter and blend the mixture very well.
3. Let the bread dough rest for around 2 to 3 hours or until you notice its size double: Make sure to put it in a plastic container or a bag.
4. Tips: Ensure that there is no wind as this may dry up the dough. Also, the longer you proof the bread, the softer it will be - so no shortcuts! Nevertheless, a warmer kitchen can help to speed up the time needed for the proofing.
5. Now, divide your obtained dough into small balls of 30g each.
6. Prepare an egg wash by combining the egg of a yolk with 1 tbsp of milk.
7. With your hands, shape every ball and the place the number of balls you obtain just in one baking paper.
8. Add the pumpkin seeds on top of the dough or you can use sesame too.
9. Brush your balls with the egg wash that you have already prepared.

10. Now, all that is left to do is to let the dough rest again for 30 minutes.
11. Pour 1 ½ cups of water into your Instant Pot
12. Place a trivet in the bottom of your Instant Pot; then Place your dough balls in a sprayed tray and cover with an aluminum foil
13. Close the lid of your Instant Pot and set seal the valve
14. Set the timer for about 20 minutes and pressure cook the bread
15. When the pressure cooking is done, do a quick pressure release method; then when it is safe to do, open the Instant Pot and remove the baking tray
16. Serve and enjoy your bread!

Nutrition Information

Calories: 252.9| Fat: 7.4g | Carbohydrates: 45.1g| Fiber: 1.1g |Protein: 2.8g

Recipe 121: Cranberry Bread

TIME TO PREPARE:
15 minutes

COOK TIME
30 Minutes

SERVING
6 People

Ingredients

- 2 ¼ cups of white whole wheat flour
- 1 cup of white flour
- 2 tablespoons of vital wheat gluten
- 1 ½ teaspoons of salt
- 1 teaspoon of instant yeast
- 1 ½ cups of room temperature water
- ½ cup of pecans, whole and chopped
- ½ cup of cranberries

Instructions

1. In a large bowl, mix together the wheat flour, the white flour, the wheat gluten, the salt, and the yeast.
2. Add in the water and with your bare hands, combine until you get an incorporated dough; if the dough is sticky; sprinkle 2 tablespoons of flour on top and fold it it
3. Place the dough on a parchment paper; then put inside your Instant pot liner
4. Lock the lid of the Instant Pot and seal the valve
5. Press the setting function yogurt, then adjust until you see the display 24:00 and adjust the timer to 4:30
6. Wait for the beeper to indicate that the cycle has started and after about 4 hours
7. Grab the sides of the parchment paper to lift the dough; then pat the dough into a rectangular shape

and sprinkle with the cranberries and the pecans
8. Pull the edges of your dough on top of the cranberries and pecans
9. Place back into the center of the parchment paper; then in your Instant Pot and secure the lid
10. Place a 6 to 8 cast iron pot in your oven with the lid on
11. Preheat your oven to 450°F and after about 30 minutes, remove the pot from the oven and place the lid to the side
12. Lift the dough from the pot and place it in the cast iron pot and put inside the oven
13. Bake for about 30 minutes
14. Remove the lid of the pot; then bake for about 15 additional minutes
15. Remove from the oven; then hold the corners of the paper very well
16. Place the bread over a cooling rack; then serve and enjoy your bread!

Nutrition Information

Calories: 130| Fat: 4.4g | Carbohydrates: 36.2g| Fiber: 3.8g |Protein: 5.5g

Recipe 123: Cheddar Cheese Bread

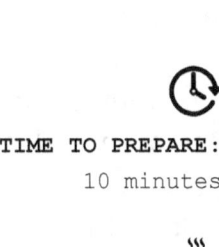

TIME TO PREPARE:
10 minutes

COOK TIME
65 Minutes

SERVING
4 People

Ingredients

- 1 bottle of beer
- 3 cups of self rising flour
- 2 tbsp of melted salted butter
- 1 can of diced chiles optional, about 4 oz.
- ½ cup of shredded cheddar cheese

Instructions

1. In a large bowl; pour a bottle of beer in; then gently mix with the flour
2. Pour in the melted butter and gently fold in
3. Spray a pan with non stick cooking spray
4. Pour the beer bread mixture in; then cover with a paper towel; then a tinfoil
5. Pour 2 cups of water in your Instant Pot pressure cooker; then put a trivet in
6. Lower the pan on the trivet and close the lid of the Instant Pot
7. Seal the valve and set the pressure cooking time to about 65 minutes at High pressure
8. Allow the pressure to naturally release
9. Flip the bread to a cutting board; then cut into pieces
10. Serve and enjoy the bread with dip of your choice!

Nutrition Information

Calories: 171| Fat: 5g | Carbohydrates: 24| Fiber: 1g |Protein: 5g

Recipe 124: Chocolate Bread

TIME TO PREPARE:
8 minutes

COOK TIME
60 Minutes

SERVING
5 People

Ingredients

- ¾ cup of whole wheat flour
- ¾ cup of white flour
- ½ tsp of baking powder
- 1 tsp of baking soda
- 1/3 cup of brown sugar
- 1/3 cup of white sugar
- ½ tsp of salt
- 1 Large egg
- ½ cup of canola oil
- 2 Small, peeled and mashed ripe bananas
- 1 Shredded small zucchini

Instructions

1. Grease a 6-cups Bundt pan and keep it aside.
2. In a large bowl, mix all together the flours, the sugars, the baking powder, the baking soda and the salt.
3. In a separate bowl, add the egg, the oil and the banana and beat until very well combined.
4. Add the flour mixture; then mix very well until your ingredients are very well combined.
5. Gently, add in the chocolate chips and the zucchini
6. Place your mixture into the prepared pan; then with a piece of foil, cover the top of your pan.
7. Place a steamer trivet in the bottom of your Instant Pot and pour in the water.
8. Put the pan over the trivet; then secure the lid and turn to "Sealed" position
9. Cook on "Manual" with a "High Pressure" For about

- 1 cup of semi sweet mini chocolate chips
- 1 cup of water

    60 minutes
10. Press the button "Cancel"; then do a natural release method
11. Remove the lid of your Instant Pot; then transfer the pan to a wire rack and let cool for about 10 minutes
12. Invert the bread and cut into slices; then serve and enjoy the bread!

Nutrition Information

Calories: 122| Fat: 2g | Carbohydrates: 24| Fiber: 1g |Protein: 3g

Recipe 125: Apple Bread

TIME TO PREPARE:
8 minutes

COOK TIME
70 Minutes

SERVING
6 People

Ingredients

- 3 Cups of cubed and peeled apple
- 1 cup of sugar
- 2 large eggs
- 1 tbsp of vanilla
- 1 tbsp of apple pie spice
- 2 cup of flour
- 1 tbsp of butter
- 1 tbsp of baking powder

Instructions

1. Mix the eggs, the butter, the cream, the sugar and the pie sauce with a mixer
2. Mix until you get a fluffy and velvety texture; then add the apples into the creamy mixture
3. Mix the flour and the baking powder
4. Add the mixture to the creamy mixture; then pour the batter into the pan and place the pan over the trivet in your Instant Pot
5. Add 1 cup of water to your Instant Pot
6. Set your Instant Pot to "Manual" at High pressure for about 70 minutes
7. Do a quick release pressure method
8. Top with the icing; then serve and enjoy your bread!

Nutrition Information

Calories: 121.2| Fat: 1g | Carbohydrates: 26.4| Fiber: 0.6g |Protein: 2.1g

Recipe 126: Pumpkin seeds bread

TIME TO PREPARE:
10 minutes

COOK TIME
50 Minutes

SERVING
6 People

Ingredients

- 3 Cups of wheat flour
- 3 Tablespoons of sugar
- 1 Cup of warm fresh milk
- 3 Tablespoons of butter
- 1/3 of an egg
- 1 tbsp of yeast
- ½ tbsp of salt

Instructions

1. Combine your ingredients all together except for the butter. Keep mixing your components on a hard surface like marble and use the palms of your hand to make it smooth.
2. Add the butter and blend the mixture very well.
3. Let the bread dough rest for around 2 to 3 hours or until you notice its size double: Make sure to put it in a plastic container or a bag.
4. Tips: Ensure that there is no wind as this may dry up the dough. Also, the longer you proof the bread, the softer it will be - so no shortcuts! Nevertheless, a warmer kitchen can help to speed up the time needed for the proofing.
5. Now, divide your obtained dough into small balls of 30g each.
6. Prepare an egg wash by combining the egg of a yolk with 1 tbsp of milk.
7. With your hands, shape every ball and the place the number of balls you obtain just in one baking paper.
8. Add the pumpkin seeds on top of the dough or you can use sesame too.
9. Brush your balls with the egg wash that you have already prepared.

10. Now, all that is left to do is to let the dough rest again for 30 minutes.
11. Place your dough balls in a tray sprayed with cooking spray; then pour 1 ½ cups of water in your Instant pot and place the trivet in it
12. Place the tray on the trivet; and cover it with a paper towel and aluminum foil
13. Close the lid of the Instant Pot and set the timer to 50 minutes and the pressure to High
14. When the timer beeps; do a quick release pressure; then slice the bread; and serve with your breakfast
15. Enjoy your bread!

Nutrition Information

Calories: 121.2| Fat: 1g | Carbohydrates: 26.4| Fiber: 0.6g |Protein: 2.1g

Recipe 127: Cornbread

TIME TO PREPARE:
9 minutes

COOK TIME
25 Minutes

SERVING
5-6 People

Ingredients

- 1 and ½ cups of yellow cornmeal
- 1 cup of frozen corn, thawed
- 2/3 cup of flour
- 2/3 cup of sugar
- 1 tbsp of baking powder
- 2 tsp of salt
- 2 large eggs
- 1 cup of buttermilk
- ¼ cup of sour cream
- ¼ cup of melted butter
- 1 cup of water
- 2 tbsp of honey

Instructions

1. Grease a round pan of about 7inches with cooking spray and keep it aside
2. In a medium bowl, mix all together the corn, the cornmeal, the flour, the sugar, the baking powder and the salt.
3. In a separate bowl; add in the eggs, the buttermilk; the cream and the butter and beat until you get a very well combined mixture
4. Add in the flour mixture and beat; then keep aside for about 10 to 15 minutes.
5. Place the mixture into the prepared pan.
6. Place a steamer trivet in the bottom of an Instant Pot; then pour in the water.
7. Place the pan on top of the trivet.
8. Secure the lid and turn it to "Seal" position.
9. Cook on the setting function "Manual" with "High Pressure" for about 23 to 25 minutes.
10. Press the button "Cancel"; then do a quick release pressure
11. Transfer the bread pan to a wire rack and let rest for about 10 minutes; then slice the bread

12. Carefully, invert to a wire rack; then cut into slices
13. Serve and enjoy your cornbread warm.

Nutrition Information

Calories: 75.4| Fat: 2g | Carbohydrates: 12.3| Fiber: 0.7g |Protein: 1.9g

CONCLUSION

For the professional cooks and experts, this book offers you a new way to look at your food. Rather than slave away when preparing your classic dinner, you can cut back time and still enjoy the flavors and textures that you want in your food. The way I see it, the recipes in this book offer you a win-win situation in terms of freshness, flavor and texture every time you prepare a meal.

If you don't have an instant pot yet you might want to consider going on the internet and carrying out extensive research to determine what works best for you it is not always the most expensive device that would deliver the best services to you you have to look at what is most important to you like the kinds of meals that you prepare if you are the type of person who loves to be in the kitchen and so on when you find the right instant pot for your kitchen the possibilities are endless

While we have catalogued a variety of instant pot meals to change and transform dinner time or breakfast time at home, there is still so much you can do. Food can be an art. We already know that food is vital everyday living and if you want to stay healthy, you would also need to pay attention to the process in which your food is prepared. And that is what the instant pot is there for.

But something that I will always say in any of my cookbooks… you are meant to have fun with the process always. All the serious things about food are great but if you really want to enjoy your food and your cooking, you need to learn to have fun with it. So, as you go on to enjoy the recipes I've shared with you, remember to enjoy the process.